*Christmas Treasures*

# Christmas Treasures

*by*

## J. HAROLD GWYNNE

*Author of*

PASSION FLOWERS
THE GOSPEL OF CHRISTMAS
IN PRAISE OF MOTHERS
MOTHERS AND THEIR SONS
HE SPAKE IN PARABLES

WM. B. EERDMANS PUBLISHING CO.

Grand Rapids                    1940                    Michigan

CHRISTMAS TREASURES
*by* J. HAROLD GWYNNE

---

*This Book of Christmas is respectfully dedicated to my friend and co-worker* WILLIAM B. EERDMANS

# FOREWORD

THE KINDLY RECEPTION given to my first volume of Christmas messages entitled, *The Gospel of Christmas,* (1938) has greatly encouraged me in preparing this second volume, *Christmas Treasures,* (1940).

IT HAS BEEN MY CUSTOM for a number of years to dwell on Christmas themes during the whole month of December. Many congregations do not hear more than one or two Christmas sermons a year. As a result, the rich spiritual treasures of the Christmas Gospel are not as well known and as fully appreciated as they deserve to be. I venture the suggestion that most congregations would welcome a fuller exposition of the message of "sweetness and light" contained in the Nativity narratives.

A DISTINGUISHED CLERGYMAN recently said in my hearing that the average minister can hope to have only *one* good Christmas sermon. I believe this to be a very serious understatement of the case. Making no claim whatever that my *thirty* messages are *good,* I still insist that they point the way to the abundantly rich pastures of this field of the Scriptures. My hope is that many young ministers, especially, will form the habit of devoting more than ordinary attention to the Infancy Gospels. They will do well to do this, for I have learned from experience that some of them do not even know which two of the four Gospels contain records of the birth of Jesus!

I CHERISH THE HOPE that all humble readers of this book of Christmas will find that it, too, "exalts Him for Whom Christmas is named" and that it will inspire and encourage many to offer their treasures to the Christ Child.

J. HAROLD GWYNNE

# CONTENTS

## Part One

## Part Two

## Part Three

*Part One*

# Preparing for Christmas

# WATCHMAN, TELL US OF THE NIGHT

*Watchman, tell us of the night,*
*  What its signs of promise are:*
*Traveler, o'er yon mountain's height,*
*  See that glory-beaming star!*
*Watchman, doth its beauteous ray*
*  Aught of joy or hope foretell?*
*Traveler, yes; it brings the day,*
*  Promised day of Israel.*

*Watchman, tell us of the night;*
*  Higher yet that star ascends:*
*Traveler, blessedness and light,*
*  Peace and truth, its course portends.*
*Watchman, will its beams alone*
*  Gild the spot that gave them birth?*
*Traveler, ages are its own,*
*  And it bursts o'er all the earth!*

*Watchman, tell us of the night,*
*  For the morning seems to dawn:*
*Traveler, darkness takes its flight;*
*  Doubt and terror are withdrawn.*
*Watchman, let thy wanderings cease;*
*  Hie thee to thy quiet home.*
*Traveler, lo, the Prince of Peace,*
*  Lo, the Son of God is come!*

—JOHN BOWRING, 1825.

*11/27/49*

*12/17/50 (parts)*

# I

## PREPARING FOR CHRISTMAS

MATTHEW 3:3, *The voice of one crying in the wilderness,*
*Make ye ready the way of the Lord,*
*Make his paths straight.*

IN ANCIENT times, it was the custom of the Oriental
monarch when about to make a journey to some distant
point of the empire to send a herald before him to direct the
people to prepare roads so that their sovereign might proceed
with ease and comfort. This was especially necessary when
the monarch's journey took him into the wilderness, that is,
the vast stretches of uncultivated lands which were crossed
only by winding paths, and not by highways worthy of a
sovereign. The whole population along the line of royal
progress turned to road-making; the crooked places were
made straight; the rough ways were made smooth; the low
places were filled, and the high places cut down, so that a
straight, smooth, level highway was made ready for the royal
retinue.

This is one figure of speech from Oriental life that is
perfectly familiar to us of the Occident. The vast program
of highway construction of the past few decades has made
us very familiar with the operations of road building. It has
shown us the immense advantage of proper sub-grading by
means of cuts and fills, elimination of curves, adequate drain-
age, and so forth. A trip over some of our improved highways where dangerous curves have been eliminated, steep
grades cut down, and other improvements made serves as an
illuminating commentary on this text. We are not told
whether the Oriental monarch in making his journeys had

to contend with detours or not. If he did, we can imagine his royal ire would be so aroused that a number of innocent subjects would be beheaded as a result! At any rate, it was a wise precaution on his part to send word ahead to have the road made ready.

## I. The Coming Messiah.

This figure of speech as used originally by Isaiah is a prophecy of the coming Messiah. It is quoted in all four of the Gospels as referring to the advent of Jesus as proclaimed by the forerunner John the Baptist. Just as the Oriental monarch sends a courier to exhort the people to prepare roads, so God sends His messenger John to exhort the people to prepare their hearts for the coming of the Messiah. John the Baptist applies this prophecy to himself, saying, "I am the voice of one crying in the wilderness, Make straight the way of the Lord, as said Isaiah the prophet" (John 1:23). Thus John indicates that he is God's chosen messenger sent to be the herald of the Messiah. As such he invites and exhorts the nation of Israel to make that moral preparation of heart which is essential to the proper reception of their King.

Each year, with the coming of the birthday of the King, the glory of God is again revealed to those whose hearts are made ready to receive Him. For the Kingdom of God is ever at hand for those who are spiritually alert, and the King is ever coming to those whose hearts are highways of welcome. The great picture we have of Christ in this age in which He comes to us by His Spirit, is of One Who continually seeks a closer fellowship with His people. The Book of Revelation gives us this picture of Him, outside the door of our hearts, seeking admission: "Behold, I stand at the door and knock: if any man hear my voice and open the door, I will come in to him, and will sup with him, and he with me." Christ is ever seeking a larger place in our lives, in our churches, and in the corporate life of the nation. At each Christmas season He comes knocking at the door of countless hearts the world around, seeking a closer communion with all those who will open the door and receive Him into their lives.

## II. *Preparing the Way.*

The solemn injunction, "Prepare ye the way of the Lord," indicates that the way was not ready for the progress of the King. Had the way been ready, there would have been no need for the command to prepare the way. When Christ first came, was the way prepared for Him? A few loyal hearts were ready to receive Him, but that was all. At His birth He was cradled in a manger in Bethlehem because there was no room for Him in the inn. Herod the king trembled on his throne when he heard of Him Who was born King of the Jews, and straightway perpetrated one of the bloodiest crimes of history in the attempt to murder the innocent child Jesus. The aged Simeon told the mother that a sword would pierce her soul by reason of the treatment accorded her Son by the people of Israel. John the Evangelist summed up the whole tragic history in the words, "He came unto his own, and they that were his own received him not." Morally speaking, the heart of the nation to which Jesus came was like a wilderness, marked with many and devious paths of religious tradition and casuistry, but traversed by no great spiritual highway over which the King could travel to His rightful throne as Messiah and Lord. John the Baptist called the nation to repentance and to faith in the Son of God; but the nation did not heed, and John was beheaded. Jesus performed His public ministry in their midst and offered Himself to His people as their Messiah and King, and Him they crucified.

Nineteen centuries have elapsed, and the world has not yet received Christ as Lord and King. The message of the prophet, "Prepare ye the way of the Lord" is just as pertinent today as it was when Isaiah first uttered it, or when John the Baptist thundered it forth to the crowds along the Jordan. Many people outside the Church are just as indifferent to the claims of Christ as were the most hardened unbelievers of Jerusalem. There is much in the social, industrial, political and educational life of the nation that is not yet controlled by the principles and teachings of Christ. Within the Church itself, there are many sad examples of departure from the high ideals of genuine Christian discipleship.

Now Christ is coming again. He is always coming, for He is very gracious, patient and insistent. His heralds proclaim the message: "Prepare ye the way of the Lord," and all the people are called upon to help build the road for Him. This is the value of Christmas, that it makes Christ more real, and helps to fill the hearts of people with His Spirit and His love. The season brings with it many messages of hope and good will. It sets the joy-bells ringing in the hearts of children, and brings comfort and encouragement to all who have heavy loads to bear. It gives us fresh visions of the beauty and goodness of life; it lifts us up and sends us into the New Year with greater strength and courage. All of these beneficent influences are increased manyfold when the dear Christ enters into our hearts anew. Think what our Christmas may be if we open our hearts to Him! He is Immanuel, God with us, and we may have God with us at Christmas and all the time, if we are willing to receive Him.

We may be sure that our hearts will not be prepared unless we prepare them! It lies within our power to receive or reject the Christmas message. We shall not receive special inspiration unless we make special preparation. It is very easy to crowd Christ out, just as He was crowded out of the inn. All we have to do is to do nothing at all, or to be too busy with many things to make room for Him. It is very strange and very deplorable that we in America are usually so busy with the customs and celebrations that clutter up most of our sacred days, that we fail almost entirely to observe the real spirit of these days. Hence Christmas becomes such a burden to many people that when it is over, they say with a sigh of relief, "Well, I am glad Christmas comes but once a year!" It would be tragic indeed if Christian people in general were to allow the Christmas season to pass without having felt anew down deep in their hearts the abiding joy, peace, love and hope Christmas is intended to bring. Richard Halliburton, in his book, "The Royal Road to Romance," tells of his attempt to take a photograph of the beautiful reflecting pool in the Alhambra Court of Myrtles in Spain. He made successive attempts, but was frustrated each time by the goldfish in the pool that so agitated the water that the reflection was obscured. Even so there may be some troublesome little 'goldfish' in our lives that will keep us so agitated that the beautiful message of Christmas cannot be mirrored in our souls. If we are too busy or too self-centered, or too indifferent to the coming of the King, we will only succeed in crowding Him out. We can best prepare for His coming by centering our thoughts, our affections and our hopes in Him.

### III. The Divine Command.

The word of the prophets, Isaiah and John the Baptist, is the word of God. It is God Himself Who commands and invites: "Prepare ye the way of the Lord." It is God's authoritative command to the children of men to give the proper reception to His only begotten Son, the Saviour of the world. But God allows a man to choose for himself whether he will obey or disobey. There are consequences of eternal significance hinging upon his choice. If a man chooses to do the will of God, blessing is the result. If he chooses to disobey the will of God, judgment is the result. The King is coming whether we are ready or not! He is coming at all times by the insinuating influences of His Spirit, and He is coming at the great day in all power, glory and triumph. God invites us now in this life to accept the great gift of His love, Jesus Christ, in order that we may inherit the blessings of His eternal kingdom. If we do not accept His proffered gift of love and mercy, we are setting ourselves against the plan and purpose of God, and are bringing upon ourselves the certain judgment and doom of God upon unbelievers. God has certain ways for us to prepare the way for His Son, now and at all times. Of course, the hearts of most people are touched somewhat and mellowed by the spirit of Christmas. There are not many Scrooges who are able to resist entirely the appealing influences of the season of good will. Many generous impulses, many deeds of kindness, many expressions of good will are prompted by the spell of Christmas. But the thing that concerns us most is God's way of preparing our hearts to receive His anointed King.

The first thing God requires is repentance. Repentance involves godly sorrow for sin, confession of sin, forsaking of sin, and turning to God in righteousness. This was the substance of John the Baptist's message as he called upon Israel to prepare the way of the Lord. "Repent ye: for the kingdom of heaven is at hand." The supreme need of Israel was for repentance. Israel had the law, the covenants, the promises; but Israel lacked righteousness and true love for God. They rejected and crucified their Messiah, not because they lacked evidence of His deity, power and authority; but because of the moral condition of their hearts. They were blinded and hardened by sin and unbelief. Consequently, they received Him not when He came unto them to save them from their sins.

Christ is crowded out of the hearts of men and the affairs of nations today, not because there is any lack of evidence as to the deity of Christ or as to His rightful place as the King and Lord of all life. Men profess to have difficulties as to the accuracy and authenticity of the Bible, and of course there are honest doubters. But the real trouble lies deeper. The real trouble is moral. The hearts of men are proud and stubborn and darkened by sin and unbelief. Men do not accept Christ and His rule over their lives because they do not choose to submit their wills to His will. Their hearts are not prepared to receive Him because there is no repentance toward God nor faith toward the Lord Jesus Christ. We can prepare the way of the Lord only as we are penitent toward God for our sins, and only as we accept His terms of atonement for our sins.

Again, God requires faith in the Lord Jesus Christ. God gave His Son at the first, as a helpless little baby, to simple men and women of faith. Mary and Joseph were pious and devout souls whose hearts were filled with purest love for God. Simeon and Anna were praying people who looked for the consolation of Israel. The shepherds were simple-hearted men of faith. The Wise-men from the east were seekers after the true light which lighteth every man. The disciples who followed Him in later years, and who were willing to die for Him, believed Him to be the Christ, the Son of the living God. That is what God wants of all His children— faith in Jesus Christ. We cannot possibly prepare our hearts to receive the King without a living faith in Jesus as our Saviour and Lord. Repentance toward God and faith toward our Lord Jesus Christ—these are God's requirements of us in preparing our hearts for the adorable Child of the Manger, the Suffering Servant of the Cross, the Triumphant Lord of the Resurrection and Ascension.

I have tried to express this deeper challenge of Christmas in the following verses:

> *Adorable Child of the Manger!*
> *We kneel and we worship in love;*
> *We thrill to the strains of the music*
> *That comes from the angels above;*
> *But oh! do we give Thee our treasures—*
> *The purest and best do we bring—*
> *In cheerful and joyous devotion,*
> *To Jesus our Saviour and King?*
>
> *Adorable Child of the Manger!*
> *We hasten to come to the place,*
> *Where Mary the mother is watching*
> *The sweet baby-smile on Thy face;*
> *But oh! up that Hill, can we follow*
> *The pathway of pain Thou hast trod;*
> *And faithfully carry our crosses*
> *As Suffering Servants of God?*
>
> *Adorable Child of the Manger!*
> *The star shining down on Thee there,*
> *Enraptures the world with its beauty,*
> *And vision of hope passing fair;*
> *But oh! when will men heed its rising;*
> *From hatred and war find release;*
> *In brotherly love rise and follow,*
> *The way of the Christ—Prince of Peace?*

If we meet these requirements of God, we will not only have our own hearts prepared as a highway for the King, but we will be in a position to help make the road smooth for others, that they too may receive the King, and may know the deep and abiding message of Christmas.

*He Dwelt Among Us*

## AND ART THOU COME WITH US TO DWELL

*And art Thou come with us to dwell,*
  *Our Prince, our Guide, our Love, our Lord?*
*And is Thy name Emmanuel,*
  *God present with His world restored?*

*The heart is glad for Thee! it knows*
  *None now shall bid it err or mourn;*
*And o'er its desert breaks the rose*
  *In triumph o'er the grieving thorn.*

*Thou bringest all again; with Thee*
  *Is light, is space, is breadth and room*
*For each thing fair, beloved, and free*
  *To have its hour of life and bloom.*

*The world is glad for Thee! the heart*
  *Is glad for Thee! and all is well,*
*And fixed and sure, because Thou art,*
  *Whose name is called Emmanuel!*

—Dora Greenwell, 1874.

# II

## HE DWELT AMONG US

JOHN 1:14, *And the Word became flesh, and dwelt among us (and we beheld his glory, glory as of the only begotten from the Father), full of grace and truth.*

IN THIS profoundly significant statement we are told that Christ, the eternal Son of God, left the realm of heavenly glory and came into this world, taking upon Himself full and complete human nature. We are told that He dwelt among us. The original Greek says that "He tabernacled among us." This is a very interesting statement. It is an allusion to the great fact of Israel's early history, namely, that God dwelt in the midst of His people in the Tabernacle or Tent of Meeting. The meaning is that just as God dwelt with His people in the Tabernacle of old, so Christ, the eternal Word of God, dwelt with men in the tabernacle of the flesh, that is, complete human nature. This word "tabernacle" is used in yet another sense in the New Testament. Peter and Paul both use it as referring to the human body which is indwelt by the Holy Spirit. We have, then, this three-fold truth for our consideration: first, God tabernacled with Israel in the Tent of Meeting; second, God tabernacled with His people in His Son, clothed in human flesh; third, God tabernacles in the lives of all true believers in the person of His Holy Spirit.

## I. *The Spiritual Meaning of the Ancient Tabernacle.*

The sacred meaning of the Incarnation is enhanced by an understanding of the spiritual truths symbolized by the ancient Tabernacle. The Tabernacle proper was surrounded by an open court. The entrance to the court was at the east. In this court were two objects, namely, *the altar of burnt-offerings* and *the laver*. The altar of burnt-offerings and the sacrifices offered thereon were intended to remind the people that they had no access to God except as sinners atoned for by the shedding of blood. The laver, in which the priests washed their hands and feet before ministering at the altar or entering the sanctuary, symbolized the holiness required in the service of God.

The Tabernacle proper was divided into two compartments, namely, *the Holy Place* and *the Holy of Holies*. The Holy Place was separated from the court by a veil. In like manner, the Holy of Holies was separated from the Holy Place by a veil. This inner veil contained the figures of cherubim, indicating the presence and unapproachableness of God. The Holy Place contained three objects, namely, *the table of showbread, the golden candlestick,* and *the altar of incense*. The golden table of showbread contained twelve loaves of bread that were placed before the Lord continually, being renewed every Sabbath. These twelve loaves represented the twelve tribes of Israel, and symbolized God's bountiful provision for His people and their communion with Him in and through these bounties which were enjoyed and used in His service. The golden candelabrum or seven branched candlestick, with its seven lamps, stood for the continual worship of God and for the light of testimony continually given to the world by God's people. The pure oil that fed the lamps symbolized the Holy Spirit, Who is the source of all spiritual light and testimony. The altar of incense, which stood in the Holy Place before the veil that led into the Holy of Holies, was a symbol of the obligatory and acceptable adoration of God through prayer and worship.

The Holy of Holies contained *the ark of the testimony,* made of acacia wood and overlaid with pure gold without and within. Gold was a symbol of Deity. The ark contained *the tables of the law* which God gave to Moses on Mt. Sinai, and which indicated God's special revelation to His chosen people.

Hence the ark was called the ark of the covenant, or the ark of the testimony. The lid or covering of the ark was called *the mercy seat*. It was made of solid gold, as were the two cherubim which stood on it and were one piece with it. The cherubim stood one at each end of the ark, facing each other, spreading their wings on high so as to overshadow the mercy seat. They were symbols of the presence and unapproachableness of God Who, as King of His people, dwelt between the cherubim, uttered His voice between them, and met the representatives of His people there. The mercy seat was more than a lid for the ark. Its Hebrew name meant "a covering", in the sense of atonement. The mercy seat, therefore, was intended to remind the people of the act and place of atonement and the accomplished atonement itself, which was enacted once a year when the high priest sprinkled the blood of the sacrifice upon the mercy seat. *The curtains* of white linen which inclosed the Holy of Holies symbolized the holiness of God, and the scarlet, blue, and purple threads that adorned them likewise had a sacred significance.

We see, therefore, that the original Tabernacle was rich in meaning and spiritual truth to the people of God. It represented God's presence and glory in the midst of Israel. It represented God's character as to His deity, holiness, and mercy. It enshrined the revelation God had given in His Word. It stood for the kind of service and worship that are acceptable unto God. It reminded the people of their sinfulness and of their need for atonement through the shedding of blood. It symbolized God's guiding hand and providential leading in the lives of His people. For, as you will recall, the ark guided the movements of the Israelites like a king in the midst of his troops, leading and directing the march. When the ark moved forward, the people were to move forward. When the ark halted, the people were to halt. Someone has said that the *stops* as well as the *steps* of a good man are ordered by the Lord. Thus through the movements of the ark the stops and steps of Israel were divinely directed. And it was Israel's duty to obey the leadings of God at all times.

## II. *Jesus, the True Tabernacle.*

Just as God dwelt among His people in the original Tabernacle, so Jesus tabernacled among us in human flesh. All of the rich meaning symbolized in the Tabernacle of Israel was abundantly fulfilled in Jesus Christ. He was the True Tabernacle, just as He was the true Riven Rock, or the true Pillar of Fire, or the true Paschal Lamb. He dwelt among us and men beheld the presence and glory of God in human form. His name was called Immanuel, God with us. Men beheld His glory, the glory as of the only begotten of the Father, full of grace and truth. He was the "brightness of the Father's glory, and the express image of his person." Jesus said, "He that hath seen me hath seen the Father." This is true as to the attributes of God's character. For Jesus revealed in His person the holiness, the mercy, and the love of God. Christ is the perfect revelation of God's wisdom and truth. He came not to destroy the law and the prophets but to fulfil them. He fully reveals the will of God so that men may walk in His ways, if they choose so to walk.

Jesus tabernacled among us to show us the service that God requires and how to perform that service. He shows us that to obey is best, and that the purpose of life is to minister to the needs of the world in the spirit of sacrificial love. He offers Himself as the true Guide of life, saying to all men: "Follow me; I am the way, the truth, and the life; He that followeth me shall not walk in darkness, but shall have the light of life." When He tabernacled among us He entered in once for all into the Holy Place, having obtained eternal redemption. As our High Priest, He sprinkled *His own blood* upon the mercy seat, the Cross of Calvary, and made atonement for our sins that we might enter within the veil to meet the just and holy God, and know His pardon, peace, and forgiving love.

In the Prologue to his Gospel, John tells us many wonderful things concerning the divine Friend Who tabernacled among us. He was the eternal Word through Whom all things were created, and to Whom all men owe their existence. He was the "true light" coming into the world; the only source of life and light for the souls of men. He came as a Pilgrim sojourning among His pilgrim people, sharing their nature, their life, their joys and sorrows, their temptations and sufferings, their burdens and hopes. He became a Man in order that He might be a friend and brother, a helper and Saviour to all men. While He was clothed with the glory of the only begotten Son of God, yet He chose to lay aside His heavenly glory in taking upon Himself our human nature. John and Paul both assert this truth. John records the intercessory prayer of Jesus, in which Jesus prayed to the Father that He might once more receive the glory which He had with the Father before the world was. And Paul, writing to the Philippians, said that Jesus "existing in the form of God, . . . emptied himself, taking the form of a servant, being made in the likeness of men." Paul also wrote to the Corinthians these words: "For ye know the grace of our Lord Jesus Christ, that, though he was rich, yet for your sakes he became poor, that ye through his poverty might become rich."

Thus we are told of our Lord's condescension and humiliation that were incident to His Incarnation. Nevertheless, Jesus, Who tabernacled among us, did reveal the glory of God; as much of that glory as men could bear. John says this glory consisted of His fulness of grace and truth. The essential glory of Jesus was the mark of divine Sonship impressed upon His entire human life and His life of intimate communion with the Father which so profoundly distinguished Him from every other human life. This glory was of course revealed in the miraculous works which Jesus performed, in His words of grace and wisdom, in His life of perfect holiness and sacrificial love. In the same paragraph John says Jesus was "full of grace and truth," and that "grace and truth came through Jesus Christ." Both words are rich in meaning. Grace suggests the divine love which gives itself in saving power to those who are unworthy of this love. Truth is the reality of spiritual things brought to light. It is God fully unveiled and revealed. Jesus, therefore, is God given in saving love; God fully revealed in a human life. And that we may know there is yet a glory of God unrevealed, reserved in heaven for us, John adds, "No man hath seen God at any time; the only begotten Son, who is in the bosom of the Father, he hath declared him."

John not only gives this wonderful testimony to Jesus in his Prologue, but he also describes the effects of this testimony upon those to whom it was first given. In some the testimony produced faith, and issued in abundant life. "But as many as received him, to them gave he the right to become children of God, even to them that believe on his name." John further states the issue of faith in the spiritual life of believers in these words: "For of his fulness we all received, and grace for grace." All that Christ is in His own divine person, all that He makes known concerning God the Father, all that He has done for the salvation of the world is imparted to those who believe on His name. He tabernacled among us in order that we might know God and be filled with all the fulness of God.

## III. *The Holy Spirit Tabernacles in Believers.*

God tabernacled with His people in the symbolism of the Old Testament, and He tabernacled with His people in His only begotten Son. Now, according to the clear teaching of the New Testament, He tabernacles in the life of every true believer by His Holy Spirit. This is the most intimate and personal way God has ever communed with His children. God Himself dwells within us, making our souls the tabernacles of the Holy Spirit. This signifies that the meaning and purpose of the first tabernacle and the higher truth of the Incarnation become glorious realities of Christian experience. It is through the life-giving influences of the Spirit of God that Christians receive His fulness, and grace for grace.

Two things are required of those who would have the Spirit of God tabernacle in their hearts. The one is holiness and the other is submission to the will of God. The Old Testament Tabernacle stood for the holiness of God and for the holiness of all service pertaining to God. So God says to all of His people: "Ye shall be holy; for I am holy." It takes a long time for most Christians to give up their sins and to surrender their hearts and wills completely to Christ. Our lives are not as pure and holy as they ought to be. They are not as holy as they may become, if we will yield to the sway of God's Holy Spirit. The tabernacle of old called for the obedience of Israel in all of her movements. So we are called to obey the promptings of the Holy Spirit, and to yield our lives to His sovereign control.

There is one other great truth that belongs in this message. It is this. There is yet to be another tabernacling of God among His people, besides the three modes we have been considering. The Book of Revelation tells us that in the new Jerusalem, the City of God, the redeemed shall stand in the very presence of God Himself. "Behold, the tabernacle of God is with men, and he will dwell with them, and they shall be his people, and God himself shall be with them, and be their God." This is the glorious consummation of our salvation in Jesus Christ our Lord. He has won the victory that shall bring this hope to certain fulfilment. He gave up His glory above to tabernacle with us for a little while, that through His perfect obedience and sacrifice we might be with Him in glory for eternity.

May the glad Christmas season that commemorates His birth bring these truths to our remembrance and find us ready to give Him a larger place in our love and service. And may this be our stedfast hope and prayer:

> *"Lord Jesus, King of Paradise,*
> *O keep me in Thy love,*
> *And guide me to that happy land*
> *Of perfect rest above;*
> *Where loyal hearts and true*
> *Stand ever in the light,*
> *All rapture through and through,*
> *In God's most holy sight."*

*The Christmas Message*

# HARK, THE GLAD SOUND!

*Hark, the glad sound! the Saviour comes,*
*The Saviour promised long:*
*Let every heart prepare a throne,*
*And every voice a song.*

*On Him the Spirit, largely poured,*
*Exerts its sacred fire;*
*Wisdom and might, and zeal and love,*
*His holy breast inspire.*

*He comes, the prisoners to release,*
*In Satan's bondage held;*
*The gates of brass before Him burst,*
*The iron fetters yield.*

*He comes, from the thick films of vice*
*To clear the mental ray,*
*And on the eye-balls of the blind*
*To pour celestial day.*

*He comes, the broken heart to bind,*
*The bleeding soul to cure;*
*And with the treasures of His grace*
*To enrich the humble poor.*

*Our glad hosannas, Prince of Peace,*
*Thy welcome shall proclaim;*
*And heaven's eternal arches ring*
*With Thy beloved Name.*

—REV. PHILIP DODDRIDGE, 1735.

## III

## THE CHRISTMAS MESSAGE

MATTHEW 1:23, *Behold, the virgin shall be with
child, and shall bring forth a son. And they
shall call his name Immanuel; which is, being
interpreted, God with us.*

TO THOSE who are engaged in the quest of the spiritual
life, Christmas gives a note of certainty to all of the
aspirations and affirmations of the human soul. As the many
beautiful lessons of Christmas time sink deeper into our
hearts with the passing years, we, too, can say in the words
of Tennyson: "I know, because I have felt." Christmas,
with its surpassing wealth of sentiment, beauty, light and
love, inevitably sweeps like a great flood across the world
overflowing the hearts of the people. It is futile and vain to
think of checking this flood. One who attempts to do so places
himself in the absurd position of the vexed and angry king of
the long ago who stood on the shore and lashed the sea with
vicious strokes because it would not recede at his command!

One of the strangest episodes of the first World War that
I have read about was an event that took place on a Christmas
eve out in the trenches bordering No-Man's-Land, when
some British soldiers, unable to restrain their feelings, burst
forth in the singing of Christmas carols. Presently the German soldiers in the opposite trenches joined in the singing,
and it was not long before the soldiers on both sides scram-
bled out of the trenches and gathered together out in No-
Man's-Land to exchange greetings and to share their meagre
supplies with one another. When the commanding officers
learned what had happened, they ordered their men back to

the trenches, and the next day the unwilling hostility was resumed. But for those few brief moments *the spirit of Christmas had triumphed*. It had gripped the hearts of those men whose business it was to kill each other; it had brought to the barren wastes of No-Man's-Land the song of the angels with its message of peace on earth, good will toward men. Love had triumphed over hate, and the manger lullaby had for a time drowned out the noise of battle.

The spirit of Christmas cannot be restrained! The sceptics, agnostics, and infidels may proclaim their doubts, denials, and blasphemies, but the world will go on singing with joyous and triumphant faith:

> *Hark! the herald angels sing,*
> *"Glory to the new-born King;*
> *Peace on earth, and mercy mild,*
> *God and sinners reconciled."*

The world will never let die the songs that enshrine the tenderest sentiments, the fondest hopes, and the most blessed assurances of the human heart. The world will never cease to return to the manger of Bethlehem and to kneel there in adoration, worship, and praise.

## I. A Message of Fulfillment.

The good news of Christmas is a message of fulfillment in the highest possible sense. The birth of the Saviour marked not only the fulfillment of inspired prophecy, but also the fulfillment of the highest hopes of the human race. For many weary centuries the hope of the coming Messiah had been cherished in the hearts of the Chosen People. Fifteen hundred years before the appointed time, Moses had foreseen that God would raise up a prophet from the midst of Israel like unto himself. About the same time the beautiful words of Balaam's prophecy were written:

> *I see him, but not now;*
> *I behold him, but not nigh:*
> *There shall come forth a star out of Jacob,*
> *And a sceptre shall rise out of Israel.*

Many centuries passed, and the hope which had been kept alive through all the years of Israel's troublous history was given a more definite expression by the prophet Micah:

*And thou Bethlehem, land of Judah,*
*Art in no wise least among the princes of Judah:*
*For out of thee shall come forth a governor,*
*Who shall be shepherd of my people Israel.*

How clearly the seers of God's chosen people apprehended the manner of the Messiah's coming or the nature of His redemptive work, we need not discuss now. The fact is that all of their hopes for the true salvation of Israel were centered in His coming and in His reign. We must never forget that their prophecies were not abstract predictions merely, but were inspired utterances based upon their *felt needs*. The law was not enough, sacrifices were not sufficient, prophets, priests, and kings were not an end in themselves. All of these elements that were so vital to the religion of Israel were yet only types of that which was to come. Israel yet needed One Who could complete all of these things typified, and fulfil all of the promises God had given to His people of old. With all that had gone before, Israel yet felt the need for a Saviour; for One Who could eternally save His people from their sins. The Evangelist sums up the whole matter when he says, "The law was given through Moses; grace and truth came through Jesus Christ."

But the people of Israel were not alone in their desire for a clear, an authoritative, and a complete revelation from God. The Gentile races were likewise cherishing hopes of the coming of a Redeemer. Perhaps this is the greatest lesson to be learned from the visit of the Wise Men, namely, that these mysterious visitors from the far east who were Gentiles were looking for the coming of a heaven-born child. When at last they saw His star in the east, they set forth on their long pilgrimage to seek and to find Him in Bethlehem of Judea. These Wise Men of the east represented the highest and best in the religion of the Gentile world and yet they, too, felt the need for a Saviour.

Nearly four hundred years before the birth of Christ, at the very height of Greek philosophy, art, and drama, the great Socrates said: "We must wait until some one comes from God to instruct us how to behave toward the divinity and toward men." And Socrates' noble successor, Plato, said: "It is necessary that a law-giver be sent from Heaven to instruct us. Oh, how greatly do I desire to see that man and to know who he is."

Thornton Wilder in his book, THE WOMAN OF ANDROS, tells a curious story of life and love on a small island in the Aegean Sea inhabited by Greek people at a time prior to the Christian era. Our interest in the story in this connection lies in this, that the author gives a true picture of the souls of his characters and of the emptiness of their lives. He describes their attitudes toward life, love, and death and their deep longing for something higher and better and more sure with regard to the true meaning and purpose of life. This deep longing is expressed by the Woman of Andros, as she reflects upon the emptiness and uncertainty of her life, in these poignant words: "Yet oh! if only we had some help in these matters. If only the gods were sometimes present among us. To have nothing to go by except this idea, this vague idea, that there lies the principle of living!" The author succeeds in showing how empty, vain, and transitory life was for those people without the light of true revelation to guide and comfort them. He also suggests that the uncertain gropings and deep longings of these people were to be fulfilled with the coming of Christ. For he concludes his book as he had begun it with the suggestive words: "And in the East the stars shown tranquilly down upon the land that was soon to be called Holy and that even then was preparing its precious burden!"

These references merely suggest, they do not tell us the whole sad truth of what must have been the deep, pathetic longings that pervaded the world before Christ came. No wonder His coming was heralded by angels as good tidings of great joy which should be to all the people! His coming meant that God had answered the universal cry of human need. Now all men could know that God so loved the world, that He gave His only begotten Son, that whosoever believeth on Him should not perish, but have eternal life. "If only the gods were sometimes present among us" was the great cry of a world in darkness. And then He came—Jesus Who was called Immanuel, God with us. With His coming, the hopes and dreams of Israel, the longings and aspirations of the Gentiles, and the needs of the whole world were answered and fulfilled. Phillips Brooks expressed a great truth when he said:

*The hopes and fears of all the years*
*Are met in Thee to-night.*

## II. *A Message of Peace and Good Will.*

The Gospel of Christmas is likewise a message of peace and good will to all mankind. The hymn sung by the angels over the plains of Bethlehem was a hymn of glory and of peace. This song followed the announcement of the birth of a Saviour, Christ the Lord. It was the birth of Jesus Christ that ushered in the better day of peace on earth and good will toward men.

Christ came to reveal the Fatherhood of God. He came to proclaim God's love-message to the world, and to show mankind that they are the children of God. He came to teach mankind that in acknowledging the Fatherhood of God and the Saviourhood of Christ, the world could become a true Brotherhood of men. This Brotherhood can only be builded upon His teachings; upon His spirit of love, peace, and good will.

It is only as mankind ascribes glory to God in the highest, and acknowledges the Fatherhood of God and the Sonship of Christ that peace and good will can come to the earth. We must begin where the angels began, that is, in recognizing the sovereignty of God, before we can regard all men as brothers. We must believe in Christ and be filled with His compassion and love for our fellowmen, before we can exercise the spirit of unfailing good will toward them.

Is there anything that is more needed in the world today than a universal spirit of good will? To displace the suspicion and hatred that exists between nations; to wipe out age-old racial prejudices and animosities; to break down superficial class distinctions and social barriers; to absolve religious intolerance and distrust; to sweep away the hundred petty jealousies, animosities, and prejudices that cling like burrs to our selfish lives,—the world needs to be filled with the angelic music of peace on earth, good will among men.

The angels were not mistaken about the message they brought. Christ came that men through Him might find peace with the God of heaven, and might live in peace with their fellowmen upon earth. Acceptance of Jesus Christ and obedience to His teachings is the only way to find peace with God and to live peaceably with all men. In all of our relationships one with another, we can find true harmony, accord, and happiness only as our lives are fed with the springs of good will whose source is in Christ. God be praised that the message of Christmas does make possible in a real and permanent sense the renewal and change spoken of in these touching verses by Charles Mackay, taken from his poem, "Under the Holly Bough":

> *Ye who have scorned each other,*
> *Or injured friend or brother,*
> *In this fast fading year;*
> *Ye who, by word or deed,*
> *Have made a kind heart bleed,*
> *Come gather here.*
>
> *Let sinned against, and sinning,*
> *Forget their strife's beginning,*
> *And join in friendship now:*
> *Be links no longer broken,*
> *Be sweet forgiveness spoken,*
> *Under the Holly Bough.*

## III. A Message of Invitation.

The glad tidings of Christmas come to all of us as a message of invitation. It is a message of invitation issued to all humanity by humanity's God to accept His precious Christmas gift to the world. It is an invitation to all people to receive, worship, and serve the Christ who was cradled in a manger, Who died on a cross, Who rose from the grave, Who ascended to the throne and Who lives and reigns for evermore.

Why were those simple and magnificent scenes enacted at His coming, if not to teach us how we are to receive the King? The shepherds came in simple faith and trust, believing that God had made known to them the message of the birth of One Who was to be a Saviour to all the people. And they came, not laden with rich and costly gifts (they were too poor for that), but with their honest hearts filled with love, homage, and praise to God for His wonderful gift. They knelt and worshipped Heaven's Incarnate Life to teach us and all men for ever to adore Him for His manger lowliness. The Kings of the East came bringing their precious gifts of gold, frankincense, and myrrh to express their homage and worship to the King of Kings, and to teach all men that Christ is worthy to receive the richest treasures of their lives and the true homage of their souls.

The Nativity scenes, the bright and the dark, depict the two attitudes that mankind has always had toward the Son of God — the attitude of acceptance and the attitude of rejection. Jesus constantly met these attitudes while He was upon earth. Some received Him; many rejected Him. The same is true in the modern world. Some follow the example of the Shepherds and the Wise Men and receive Him as their Saviour and King. Others follow the example of the innkeeper of Bethlehem and of Herod, and reject Him either by sheer indifference or by hostile opposition. Whether by indifference, neglect, or by hatred and active opposition the offense is the same: the Christ Child is shut out.

The winsome invitation of the Christmas message should constrain us to open our hearts to receive the Saviour and crown Him King in our lives. To do this is to accept God's great offer of mercy, forgiveness, and love expressed in the gift of His only begotten Son, the Saviour of the world. To do this is to realize the gracious promise: "as many as received him, to them gave he the right to become the children of God, even to them that believe on his name."

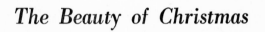

*The Beauty of Christmas*

# A THOUSAND YEARS HAVE COME AND GONE

*A thousand years have come and gone,*
*And near a thousand more,*
*Since happier light from heaven shone*
*Than ever shone before:*
*And in the hearts of old and young*
*A joy most joyful stirred,*
*That sent such news from tongue to tongue*
*As ears had never heard.*

*Then angels on their starry way*
*Felt bliss unfelt before,*
*For news that men should be as they,*
*To darkened earth they bore;*
*So toiling men and spirits bright*
*A first communion had,*
*And in meek mercy's rising light*
*Were each exceeding glad.*

*And we are glad, and we will sing,*
*As in the days of yore;*
*Come all, and hearts made ready bring,*
*To welcome back once more*
*The day when first on wintry earth*
*A summer change began,*
*And, dawning in a lowly birth,*
*Uprose the Light of man.*

*For trouble such as men must bear*
*From childhood to fourscore,*
*He shared with us, that we might share*
*His joy for evermore;*
*And twice a thousand years of grief,*
*Of conflict, and of sin,*
*May tell how large the harvest sheaf*
*His patient love shall win.*

—REV. THOMAS T. LYNCH, 1868.

IV

## THE BEAUTY OF CHRISTMAS

ISAIAH 33:17, *Thine eyes shall see the king in his beauty.*

"A THING of beauty is a joy for ever." The poet John Keats did not have Christmas in mind when he wrote this immortal line, but its truth applies to Christmas just the same. Christmas is "a thing of beauty" and "a joy for ever." It is beautiful in its origin and in its abiding significance. It is beautiful as to the sentiments it stirs within our hearts, and as to the spirit of joy and good will it brings to the world. Christmas is a thing of surpassing beauty with respect to many of its customs and observances, and the happy occasions it makes possible. So we are right in thinking of Christmas as possessing many kinds, many degrees of beauty. But the real Christmas, "the heart of the jewel" of Christmas has a beauty of infinite loveliness — a beauty all its own. It is by reason of this intrinsic beauty that Christmas will continue to bring joy to the world as long as time shall endure.

### I. *The Beauty of Simplicity.*

The beauty of Christmas is the beauty of Simplicity. The most beautiful things of the world and of life are the simplest things. This principle is woven into the very texture of the universe. Beauty is simplicity; simplicity is beauty. It is true in Nature. What is the most beautiful thing you can think about in the world of Nature? Is it a flower? a tree? a landscape? a stream? a waterfall? a mountain? the clouds? the starry heavens? a sunset sky? Whatever it may be, the thing that possesses the most exquisite beauty for you will be found to possess the native simplicity and charm that characterize the masterpieces of Nature's handiwork. It is true in painting. Consider some of the world's greatest paintings and you will find that all of them express the quality of simplicity. This is true of Millet's "The Angelus"; Raphael's "Sistine Madonna"; Da Vinci's "The Last Supper"; Hoffman's "Christ In Gethsemane"; Whistler's "Portrait of the Artists's Mother." It is likewise true of sculpture and architecture. The Lincoln Memorial at Washington, D.C., is one of the most beautiful architectural designs in this country. What is the secret of its marvellous beauty? The sheer simplicity of its construction. It is not unlike the Parthenon of ancient Athens, the most beautiful architectural achievement of "the glory that was Greece".

It is preeminently true in human language. The most beautiful gems of prose and poetry are models of simplicity. Take the Twenty-third Psalm. It contains 118 words in the Authorized Version. Of these 118 words, 90 of them are words of one syllable, and all of the 118 are words that everybody understands. Or take Tennyson's beautiful poem "Crossing the Bar", and we find that its beauty and charm consist in the consummate art of simplicity. The same is true of Lincoln's "Gettysburg Address" which is studied in our schools as a model of perfect simplicity of English composition. Again, the Parables of Jesus which stand supreme among the stories of the world are simplicity itself. "Another parable spake he unto them; The Kingdom of heaven is like unto leaven, which a woman took, and hid in three measures of meal, till the whole was leavened." Thus we discover the universal principle that beauty in its highest expression is linked with the quality of simplicity.

It is not surprising, therefore, to find the same true of Christmas. As we think of the scenes of the Nativity the thing that impresses us is their artless simplicity. The manger, the swaddling clothes, the shepherds, all belong to the lowly, commonplace things of life. Shortly before Christmas in 1934 we saw in the News Reels the picture of a cradle prepared for a new-born royal child in Europe. The cradle was a magnificent affair. No pains had been spared to make it rich and elegant in all of its appointments. The cradle when completed cost over $5,000.00. This was prepared for some infant of royal birth in our day. But what kind of cradle was prepared for the child Jesus, the King of Kings, the Son of God? There was no cradle at all prepared for Him. The mother had to use what she could find at hand. There was no room for them in the inn so they were compelled to take refuge in a stable. There the mother brought forth her first-born Son and with her own hands wrapped him in swaddling clothes and laid him in a manger.

But God the Father knew what He was about. Humble people of all lands and ages can come to the manger to worship; but not many would feel comfortable by a cradle of luxury and magnificence prepared for earth's royalty.

So much for the external simplicity. Let us look deeper into the spiritual simplicity of Christmas. Theologians speak profoundly of the doctrine of the Incarnation, and the Church has had many controversies down through the years over the question of the divine and human elements in the person of Jesus. These are important matters to be sure. But we do not think of Christmas in terms of 'Incarnation' or doctrines concerning the person of Jesus. We think of a little baby coming into the world as we came into the world and as our children come into the world. ("I believe . . . in Jesus Christ His only Son our Lord; who was conceived by the Holy Ghost; born of the Virgin Mary.") He is Jesus the Saviour, Christ the anointed King, Immanuel, God with us; but — sweetest mystery of all! — He is God with us as a helpless little baby that needs His mother's care and His father's protection. Therein lies the beauty of Christmas, that it came about in the divinely-human way it did. God knew that a little innocent baby is closest to the heart of the world, so He sent His son to be born of a lowly peasant mother, and was pleased to have Him cradled in a manger so that the poor and the lowly could draw near and worship. We cannot understand the mystery of the Incarnation, but we can all love the baby Jesus.

## II. *The Beauty of Music.*

The beauty of Christmas is the beauty of Music. How do we mean this? Not so much in an outward sense as in an inward sense. Music cannot be defined. It is harmony, melody, the rhythmic combination of tones, but it is infinitely more. It is part of the spiritual nature of the universe and the life of man that cannot be wholly captured or explained. Nearly all people love music. They love to create it and to hear it. They love the emotional effect good music produces in their souls. Music has a meaning and message for all the varying moods of the heart of man. Music is the language of the soul. It speaks to the soul, because it is born of the soul. Think what a blessing the ministry of music has been to the world! The editor of the Presbyterian Banner has said: "The musicians of the world are priests that serve at the altar of joy and gladden all our experiences. They help to scatter the gloom of the world and irradiate it with the sunshine of their songs. A master musician is to be ranked among the greatest benefactors of mankind. Who can measure the influence of a lyrical genius like Schubert? He visited the world as an angel from heaven and tarried in it for only a brief moment and departed, leaving behind him a sheaf of lovely lyrics that are as immortal as the dramas of Shakespeare. . . . Strike music out of the world, hush all these chords and songs, and we would go far towards silencing the joy of the world and wrapping it in unbroken gloom."

Now it is true that Christmas was attended with music. The shepherds heard the celestial music of the angel chorus, and we may be sure they carried this music with them ever afterwards. The lines of Wordsworth could easily have been spoken by one of these shepherds:

> *"The music in my heart I bore,*
> *Long after it was heard no more."*

Even so all of those humble people who received and helped to make the first Christmas had songs of joy and gratitude in their hearts.

To-day we cannot hear their Christmas music. There is no way of reproducing the actual song of the angelic choir. Nor can we recapture the note of exultation that thrilled the soul of Mary as she poured forth her song: "My soul doth magnify the Lord." But while we cannot hear the music of the first Christmas, we can imagine what it was like; we can feel how wonderful it must have been, and in so doing we can receive the spiritual elevation and consolation of its joyous melodies. For the words of Keats are especially true in this regard:

> *"Heard melodies are sweet, but those unheard*
> *Are sweeter . . . ."*

We have much beautiful music to brighten and gladden Christmas in our day. And we are very thankful for these noble hymns, carols and songs. But we feel that Christmas has a deeper music than can be captured by the composer's art; a sweeter song than can be put into words. The theme of this music is the salvation God has provided in Christ Jesus, and it comes as a song of glad tidings of great joy to all the people who receive Christ in their hearts. You have this music in your heart, and I have it in mine; but we cannot interpret it fully to each other. Only God Himself knows the music that slumbers on the harp-strings of our souls. Perhaps it can only find its full and perfect expression in the eternity of praise that awaits us and all the redeemed around the great White Throne.

### III. *The Beauty of Adoration.*

The beauty of Christmas is the beauty of Adoration. To adore is to honor, worship, love with intense devotion. Such adoration is the most beautiful posture of the soul. The Christmas story tells us of the adoration of the angels, the shepherds, the Wise-men, and of the mother herself. Their adoration centered in the Christ-child. The angels were the messengers from heaven sent to proclaim Messiah's birth, and to voice the divine approval of and pleasure in His coming. The angels adored Him as Saviour, Christ the Lord, Son of God.

The beginning and ending of their adoration was praise and glory to God for His mercy and love.

The world of art has made very familiar and precious the scenes of adoring wonder and worship by the shepherds and Wise-men. And in all of these masterpieces of inspiration and devotion, the Christ-child is the center of adoration and worship. They all teach us what Christ wants for Christmas and what rightfully belongs to Him as Saviour and King: our worship, our love, our gifts of life, possessions and service.

Undoubtedly the adoration of the mother is sweetest, tenderest and truest of all. She carried the secret of His divine and holy birth in her heart for many months, before ever the lowly shepherds knelt around His manger-cradle. Her heart was flooded with songs of adoration and joy upon receiving the wonderful tidings brought by the angel Gabriel. And when He was born, we can only dimly imagine the adoring love and ecstacy that filled her soul. The only record we have is that "The mother kept all these sayings, pondering them in her heart." Artists have portrayed the tender grace and the sweet loveliness of the Madonna's face. But again we may be sure that more has escaped their art than they have captured. Alfred Noyes in his exquisitely beautiful verses, "Slumber-Songs of the Madonna", has sympathetically portrayed the mother's tender love for her baby.

*"Sleep, little baby, I love thee;*
*Sleep, little king, I am bending over thee!*
*How should I know what to sing*
*Here in my arms as I swing thee to sleep?*

*Hushaby low,*
*Rockaby so,*

*Kings may have wonderful jewels to bring,*
*Mother has only a kiss for her king!*
*Why should my singing so make me to weep?*
*Only I know that I love thee, I love thee,*
*Love thee, my little one, sleep.*

\* \* \*

*"But now you are mine, all mine,*
*And your feet can lie in my hand so small,*
*And your tiny hands in my heart can twine,*
*And you cannot walk, so you never shall fall,*

*Or be pierced by the thorns beside the door,*
*Or the nails that lie upon Joseph's floor;*
*Through sun and rain, through shadow and shine,*
  *You are mine, all mine!"*

The mother's slumber-song suggests that we adore Him not only for the manger-lowliness, but also for the crown of thorns, the nails, the cross. Our eyes cannot behold the King in His beauty apart from the glory He won through sacrificial ministry, death and resurrection. Only when we realize that He bore the cross for us, that He died to save us from our sins unto eternal life can we render Him the true homage, adoration and worship that are His due. A young woman went to her minister to receive counsel and help in her troubles. "What do you see in life?" was the question she was asked. She replied, "Well, I suppose I see what everyone else sees — I see a question mark writ large on the rim of the horizon." To this her spiritual counsellor replied, "You should not see a question mark; you should see a cross." It is only when we see the cross and accept the cross as the means of our salvation and as the symbol of our discipleship that we can know the real beauty of the Christmas Gospel and the Christian life.

May Christmas be so real to us all that we shall indeed "see the king in his beauty", and so surrender our hearts to Him in adoration and love that the prayer of the Psalmist shall be answered in each one: "And let the beauty of the Lord our God be upon us" — now and increasingly in the days to come.

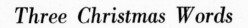

*Three Christmas Words*

# LO, GOD, OUR GOD, HAS COME!

*Lo, God, our God, has come!*
  *To us a Child is born,*
*To us a Son is given;*
  *Bless, bless the blessed morn,*
*O happy, lowly, lofty birth,*
*Now God, our God, has come to earth!*

*Rejoice! our God has come*
  *In love and lowliness:*
*The Son of God has come,*
  *The sons of men to bless.*
*God with us now descends to dwell,*
*God in our flesh, Immanuel.*

*Praise ye the Word made flesh!*
  *True God, true man is He.*
*Praise ye the Christ of God!*
  *To Him all glory be.*
*Praise ye the Lamb that once was slain,*
*Praise ye the King that comes to reign!*

—Dr. Horatius Bonar.

# V

## THREE CHRISTMAS WORDS

MATTHEW 2:10, *And when they saw the star, they rejoiced with exceeding great joy.*

THE story of Christmas has three words that stand out in great prominence, and that have become familiar and precious around the world. These three words well convey the meaning and message of Christmas, as well as the fuller meaning of the whole life and ministry of Jesus. The words are: STAR, SONG, SAVIOUR.

### I. The Star.

First, the Christmas Star. We read of the star in Matthew's account of the birth of Jesus, where it is mentioned four times. Here are the references. "Wise-men from the east came to Jerusalem saying, Where is he that is born King of the Jews? for we saw his *star* in the east, and are come to worship him" (Mt. 2:1a-2). "Then Herod privily called the Wise-men, and learned of them exactly what time the *star* appeared" (Mt. 2:7). "And they, having heard the king, went their way; and lo, the *star,* which they saw in the east, went before them, till it came and stood over where the young child was" (Mt. 2:9). "And when they saw the *star,* they rejoiced with exceeding great joy" (Mt. 2:10).

The Bethlehem Star shone down upon a world of darkness, ignorance, superstition, cynicism and despair. The condition of the times is accurately described by the words of Zacharias, who said that even the people of Israel were as those who dwelt "in darkness and the shadow of death." If this was true of the people of God, how much more was it true of the heathen world! Paul described the spiritual condition of the Gentile peoples when he said they were "alienated from the commonwealth of Israel, and strangers from the covenants of the promise, having no hope and without God in the world" (Eph. 2:12). It was an age of spiritual destitution, darkness, despair and the shadow of death. Into this world came the Star of the East with its promise of a brighter and better day.

The Bethlehem Star was a star of hope. To the Wise-men of the east, its rising marked the fulfilment of long cherished expectation and desire. These Persian Magi were probably priests of Zoroaster, and as such were worshippers of Light as opposed to the evil principle of Darkness. They studied the stars and regarded them as the "thoughts of the Eternal". They had undoubtedly read the prophecy of Balaam, uttered some fifteen centuries before: "There shall come forth a star out of Jacob, And a sceptre shall rise out of Israel" (Num. 24:17). When at last, they saw the star in the east, they knew that the time had come; and they set forth on their historic journey to Bethlehem to see this "star out of Jacob", and to find for themselves "the Light of the world".

But the Bethlehem Star was also a star of mystery, a star of evil omen. When Herod the king heard of it, he was troubled. To his wicked and cunning mind it was a sign that boded ill. His only thought was that its appearance, like the handwriting on the wall of Belshazzar's palace, presaged his downfall, and the enthronement of another as Israel's king. He was determined at all costs to exterminate this new incumbent to the throne by his customary methods of cruelty and treachery. But Herod's wicked designs came to naught, while God's purposes were fulfilled. Strange as it may seem, we cannot fail to note that the star which was a star of hope, joy and blessing to some, was at the same time a star of presentiment, trouble and judgment to others. Its benevolent meaning has always been hidden from the hostile and unbelieving. It is a sign of judgment, condemnation and defeat to wicked and sinful men. It is a portent of doom and destruction to all those who array themselves in hostile opposition to the plans and purposes of Almighty God.

Again, the Christmas Star was a star of guidance. It guided the Wise-men on their dangerous and difficult journey from the distant east to the place where they found the Christ-child. It guided their hopes, their aspirations, and their faith to Him Who was the light of the revelation of God's saving love to the Gentiles. It guided their believing hearts to prof-fer their richest gifts to the young Child, and to receive Him as their King. Even so, the Star of Bethlehem continues to be a guiding Beacon to all questing souls who are seeking the truth, the hope and the salvation that are to be found in God's gift of love to the world.

Once more, the Christmas Star was a star of joy. When the Wise-men saw the star that stood over where the young child was, they rejoiced with exceeding great joy. To them it was the joy of an accomplished quest. Their life-long search for truth and light, for purity and righteousness was satisfied. They had found something of that spiritual joy of which their King was later to speak to His subjects: "These things have I spoken unto you, that my joy may be in you, and that your joy may be made full" (Jn. 15:11). Down through the years, the joy that the Wise-men knew has been known by all those who have come "to the end of the way of the wan-dering star", and have found the answer to life's quest in God's love-gift to the world. The poet John Keats tells us of the joy and ecstacy that filled his soul upon reading for the first time the noble poetry of Homer in translation. Said he:

> *"Then felt I like some watcher of the skies*
> *When a new planet swims into his ken."*

Ever since the Star of Bethlehem shone forth as a guiding beacon-light to those royal travelers of the long ago, the world has possessed a new meaning, a new hope and a new joy. For its dawning marked the entrance of the Divine into hu-man life, the rising of the Sun of Righteousness with hope and healing in His wings.

## II. *The Song.*

The second thing is the Christmas Song. Christmas brought to the sad and joyless world a song with a message of joy, gladness and love. That message has come down through the years, in what Longfellow has called,

> *"The unbroken song*
> *Of peace on earth, good-will to men!"*

The story of Christmas is vibrant with the songs of joy and praise and blessing that came from those Celestial Beings who announced the birth of the Saviour, and from those humble men and women who received their glad tidings of great joy to all the people. The song of the Angelic Choir was a song of praise and glory to God in the highest, and of peace and good-will to men on earth. The hearts of the shepherds were singing within them, as they returned glorifying and praising God for all the things they had heard and seen. The princely Magi returned to their own country with a new song of joy in their hearts. We also have the songs of Elizabeth, Mary, Zacharias and Simeon, which were songs of joy, gratitude, faith and hope. Luke also tells the story of an old praying woman by the name of Anna who saw the infant Jesus in the temple, and whose heart was filled with songs of thanksgiving and praise. It is convincingly clear, therefore, that all who truly received the Christ of Christmas likewise possessed songs of joy and peace in their hearts.

Thus Christmas continues to bring each year, on a world-wide "hook-up", a message of joyous song that is heard by all mankind. And the central theme of all the Christmas music is the tender love and mercy of God the Heavenly Father as revealed in Christ Jesus our Lord.

God intends that this life of ours shall be one glad sweet song. This is not to say that our lives shall be free of sorrow, suffering and affliction. There is a tradition concerning the song of the nightingale, the sweetest singer of all the birds, that its song is the expression of eternal passion and eternal pain. So it is that the sweetest songs of mortals are born out of the deepest experiences of sorrow and suffering. The songs come not in spite of these things, but as a result of these things. The heart sings when it is happy, confident and free. The heart does not sing when it is heavy with doubt, fear, pessimism or despair. There are many philosophies of human life that are pessimistic, cynical and hopeless; that tend to crush all songs out of the human heart. But how different is the Christian philosophy of life! The Christian believes in God the Father Who loves and cares and delivers. He believes in a Saviour Who is an ever-present Helper, Comforter and Friend. He believes in a Heaven of eternal life and blessedness. And because he is rooted and grounded in these great realities of the Gospel, he is confident, trustful, serene. Believing in God and in Christ his Saviour, his heart is not troubled nor afraid but is filled with songs of love and joy and peace.

## III. *The Saviour.*

The third matchless word of the Christmas story is the word Saviour. This word shines out with a brilliance that transcends the glory of the guiding star of hope. It is the brightest Star in the deep blue firmament of the Christmas sky. The music of that word is sweeter by far than the songs of mortals or of angels. It is the word that expresses and that carries to the highest climax of harmony and perfection, the sweet and lovely theme of God's age-long oratorio of redemption.

We find the thought of a Saviour imbedded in the very heart of the Christmas message. When the Angel of the Lord appeared to Joseph and foretold the birth of a Son to Mary, he spake these words, "And she shall bring forth a son; and thou shalt call his name Jesus; for it is he that shall save his people from their sins" (Mt. 1:21). Again, the Angel of the Lord appeared to the shepherds by night, and said unto them, "Be not afraid: for behold, I bring you good tidings of great joy which shall be to all the people: for there is born to you this day in the city of David a Saviour, who is Christ the Lord" (Lk. 2:10-11). To the venerable Simeon, the infant Jesus appeared as "the Lord's Christ"; as "the consolation of

Israel", and as the salvation of the Lord God both for Israel and the Gentiles. (Was there ever more suggestive picture than that of this patient old saint of Israel holding in his frail and trembling arms the Salvation of God for the world, in the form of a helpless little baby?) To Anna, the devout and pious prophetess, the birth of Jesus meant "the redemption of Jerusalem". Likewise to Zacharias the priest, and to Mary the mother, the birth of Jesus marked the coming of the promised Messiah for the redemption of Israel. And so in one way or another, the various threads of the Christmas story are woven together to form the beauteous pattern of God's full and free salvation in the gift of His only begotten Son.

The world into which Christ was born needed above all else a Saviour. It was a world that had many kings, who like Herod, could only terrorize and brutalize their subjects. It was a world that had many great and mighty warriors, who only added to the bloodshed and misery among oppressed peoples. It was a world that had many philosophers, but no wisdom to guide the people in the ways of righteousness or to give them hope. It was a world of many priests and many religions, but these could not save the people from their sins. The pagan religions were incapable of uplifting and purifying the world. On the contrary, they promoted obscenity and the grossest sensuality. Even the Hebrew religion had degenerated into a cold and lifeless system of law and ritual. Prophets, priests, kings, emperors, warriors, statesmen, poets, philosophers, scribes, — all had failed to meet the deep-seated need of humanity. The world stood in dire need of a Saviour.

Into this world came One Who was to be lifted up on a Cross — Jesus the Saviour of the world. His enemies, the Pharisees, said of Him, "He receiveth sinners." They said it in scorn, but in so doing, they announced the great message of the Gospel of the compassionate Friend of sinners. "He receiveth sinners." He received them then and He receives them now. To all who come to Him, He gives His pardon, cleansing, peace and power. He saves unto the uttermost all those who come unto God through Him. His salvation is complete and perfect and eternal. He makes us new creatures in this life, and glorified sons of God in the life to come.

This Gospel of the complete and perfect salvation wrought for men by the Saviour Who came as a little babe has been well expressed in a Christmas poem by Charles Henry Crandall :—

> *"As little children in a darkened hall*
> *At Christmas-tide await the opening door,*
> *Eager to tread the fairy-haunted floor*
> *About the tree with goodly gifts for all,*
> *And into the dark unto each other call —*
> *Trying to guess their happiness before, —*
> *Or of their elders eagerly implore*
> *Hints of what fortune unto them may fall:*
> *So wait we in Time's dim and narrow room,*
> *And with strange fancies, or another's thought,*
> *Try to divine, before the curtain rise,*
> *The wondrous scene. Yet soon shall fly the gloom,*
> *And we shall see what patient ages sought,*
> *The Father's long-planned gift of Paradise."*

## Part Two

# Christmas Courage

# CALM ON THE LISTENING EAR OF NIGHT

*Calm on the listening ear of night*
*Come heaven's melodious strains,*
*Where wild Judea stretches forth*
*Her silver-mantled plains;*
*Celestial choirs from courts above*
*Shed sacred glories there;*
*And angels, with their sparkling lyres,*
*Make music on the air.*

*The answering hills of Palestine*
*Send back the glad reply,*
*And greet from all their holy heights*
*The Day-spring from on high:*
*O'er the blue depths of Galilee*
*There comes a holier calm;*
*And Sharon waves in solemn praise*
*Her silent groves of palm.*

*"Glory to God!" the lofty strain*
*The realm of ether fills;*
*How sweeps the song of solemn joy*
*O'er Judah's sacred hills!*
*"Glory to God!" the sounding skies*
*Loud with their anthems ring:*
*"Peace on the earth; good-will to men,*
*From heaven's eternal King."*

*This day shall Christian tongues be mute,*
*And Christian hearts be cold?*
*O catch the anthem that from heaven*
*O'er Judah's mountains rolled,*
*When burst upon that listening night*
*The high and solemn lay,*
*"Glory to God; on earth be peace:"*
*Salvation comes today.*

—Rev. Edmund H. Sears, 1834.

# VI

## CHRISTMAS COURAGE

LUKE 1:13, *But the angel said unto him, Fear not, Zach-*
*arias: because thy supplication is heard, and thy wife*
*Elisabeth shall bear thee a son, and thou shalt call*
*his name John.*

CHRISTMAS has a message of courage, cheer, and consolation for all. This is commonly admitted and is generally evident in the effect Christmas produces in the lives of
all kinds of people. But much of the "Christmas spirit" so-
called is superficial and fleeting. It passes away with the holiday mood and the seasonal activities peculiar to Christmas.

On the other hand, there is a deep and abiding experience
of strong courage and joyous confidence for those who realize
the real meaning of Christmas. We are led to consider this
phase of the Christmas Gospel by the fresh discovery (for us)
of a phrase that is repeated three times in Luke's account of
the Nativity. We refer to the angel's word, "Fear not" or
"Be not afraid." The practical meaning of this word of the
angel may be positively stated as follows: "Be of good courage; be comforted; be of good cheer." It is like the word of
Jesus to His disciples, "Be of good cheer, it is I; be not
afraid" (Matthew 14:27). This message of heavenly counsel
and courage was spoken by the angel to Zacharias the priest,
to Mary the virgin, and to the shepherds. Let us seek to learn
what these words meant to those to whom they were first
spoken, and what they contain in the way of spiritual guidance and help for us.

## I. To Zacharias—The Courage of Answered Prayer.

Luke's narrative concerning the parents of John the Baptist is filled with human interest and pathos. In the days of Herod, king of Judaea, there was a certain priest named Zacharias, of the course of Abijah: and he had a wife of the daughters of Aaron, whose name was Elisabeth. They were both righteous before God, walking in all the commandments and ordinances of the Lord blameless. The great sorrow of this godly couple was that they had no child to bless and comfort them in their old age. Their sorrow was deepened by the fact that they had given up hope of ever having a child.

But the old priest, Zacharias, continued his priestly service in the temple. We read in I Chronicles, chapter 24, that David had divided the priesthood into twenty-four courses, and that the course of Abijah was the eighth course. According to this plan, each course officiated for a week at a time; the weekly turn coming twice a year. There was this exception, that all of the courses were employed at the great national feasts such as the Passover and others. It was customary for the course of priests on duty to allot to the members the several functions to be performed in the daily ministrations in the sanctuary. When the course to which Zacharias belonged assembled at Jerusalem the lot fell to him to burn incense. This sacred privilege was one that a priest could enjoy only once in his lifetime, that of entering the Holy Place at the hour of prayer and there offering incense upon the golden altar just before the veil in the very presence of God. The supreme privilege and opportunity of his life had come!

As the venerable priest ministered in the Holy Place, and the whole multitude of people were praying without, a remarkable thing happened. As the cloud of incense began to rise, the true symbol of accepted petitions, there appeared to Zacharias an angel of the Lord standing on the right side of the altar of incense. The old priest was greatly troubled when he saw him, and fear fell upon him. "But the angel said unto him, Fear not, Zacharias: because thy supplication is heard, and thy wife Elisabeth shall bear thee a son, and thou shalt call his name John."

Let us look most reverently into the secret of the old man's heart, for the place on which we stand is holy ground. The faithful priest had been praying many long years for the birth of a son. He had grown old and God had not seemed to hearken unto his prayer. He continued praying, although he had evidently surrendered hope that his prayer for a son would be answered. He and his wife had grown old, and it seemed impossible that a child could be given. But Zacharias' prayer for a son was more than personal. He was really praying for the salvation of his people through the birth of a son. His prayer was spiritual and national and truly sacerdotal. The real burden of his persevering prayer is seen not only in the promised birth of a son, but in the mission of John who was "to make ready for the Lord a people prepared for him." The real prayer of the devout priest is revealed in the tender words from his song, the "Benedictus":

*"Yea and thou, child, shalt be called the prophet of the Most High:*
*For thou shalt go before the face of the Lord to make ready his ways;*
*To give knowledge of salvation unto his people*
*In the remission of their sins."*

The prayer of Zacharias, the devout priest, was answered. To him the answer seemed long in coming, but when it did come his faith did not measure up to God's requirement. For this lack of faith and show of unbelief he was stricken dumb for a season. But God was faithful, and in His own time and way answered the supplications of His faithful servant. The name Zacharias means "Jehovah hath remembered," and the name Elisabeth means "God is a covenant maker." Their very names and characters bear witness to God's graciousness and faithfulness as the Hearer and Answerer of prayer.

It is most significant to note the large place given to prayer in the Christmas story. God gave His servant John, the Forerunner of the Messiah, to godly parents in answer to prayer. After the birth of John the first words spoken by Zacharias were the words of the "Benedictus," a fervent prayer of praise and thanksgiving to God for His visitation and redemption. In like manner, the song of Mary, the "Magnificat," is a prayer of pure praise to God for His power, holiness, and mercy. In connection with the presentation of the baby Jesus in the temple by His parents, we are introduced to Simeon and Anna whose godly lives were patterns of persistent prayer. Christmas, then, begins and ends with prayer. The men and women who made Christmas possible, humanly speaking, were men and women of prayer. Those who received the spiritual gifts and blessings and rewards of Christmas received them in answer to prayer.

What was true for them will likewise be true for us. Christmas brings to all sincere, devout, prayerful hearts the assurance and consolation of answered prayer. Fear not, O thou of the anxious and troubled heart, thy supplication is heard. Take new courage and go on in the faithful performance of daily duty and God will reward thee abundantly. Continue to wait stedfastly upon Him in prayer and He will bring it to pass. Only be sure that the prayer of thine heart is for the glory of God and for the coming of the Kingdom of His dear Son. For if thou dost seek first the Kingdom of God and His righteousness, all the other needs of life will be abundantly supplied. Pray fervently and stedfastly in the name of Him for Whom Christmas is named, Christ the Lord.

## II. To Mary—The Courage of Divine Approval.

The angel Gabriel had appeared to the aged priest Zacharias amidst the splendors of the Temple in Jerusalem at the hour of prayer. Six months later he was sent to Mary the young virgin in her humble home in Nazareth of Galilee. The angel said to the virgin, "Hail, thou that art highly favored, the Lord is with thee." Mary was greatly troubled at his saying and much perplexed to know the meaning of his salutation. "And the angel said unto her, Fear not, Mary: for thou hast found favor with God." Mary's wonder and astonishment grew as she heard the angel announce that she should bring forth a son, and call his name JESUS. The angel made clear that before her marriage she was to become the mother of the Son of the Most High; the heir of the throne of David;

the ruler of the house of Jacob; the sovereign of an eternal kingdom.

The exclamation of Mary expressed astonishment but not unbelief, as she said, "How shall this be?" The angel then revealed to her the mystery of the Incarnation, saying, "The Holy Spirit shall come upon thee, and the power of the Most High shall overshadow thee: wherefore also the holy thing which is begotten shall be called the Son of God." To confirm the truth of this promise the angel "added a sign and proof in the surprising fact that Elisabeth, the aged kinswoman of Mary, was soon to be blessed with a son. This was in fulfillment of a promise made by the same angel messenger, and the marvel in the case of Elisabeth would assure Mary of the certain accomplishment of the gracious and more surprising promise to her." Mary's reply revealed her implicit faith in the word of God and her perfect submission to the will of God. "And Mary said, Behold, the handmaid of the Lord; be it unto me according to thy word." And the angel departed from Mary.

To Mary was granted the blessed assurance of divine approval. This knowledge that she was chosen to be the handmaid of the Lord and that she was to give birth to the promised Messiah and Saviour filled her soul with joy and praise and gratitude and blessing. Her song contains this personal note of God's favor upon her; then the universal note as she dwells upon God's favor and blessing to all of His humble people everywhere; then the national note as she speaks of God's faithfulness and favor to the seed of Abraham. Thus to Mary came the greatest good and highest joy of life, that of being used of God to further His redeeming purposes in the world.

To know that one is approved of God, to be assured that one is walking with God in fellowship and in obedience to God's holy will, this is the secret of courage and confidence and joy. Men and women become fearful and discouraged and uncertain when they forget God and forsake His ways and disobey His commandments. Only in His will can men find enduring confidence and lasting peace. The Christmas Gospel emphasizes the importance of being assured of divine approval in all of our plans, purposes, undertakings and relationships. The highest goal for any woman is to be a "handmaid of the Lord." The highest goal for any man is to be a servant of the Most High. This goal can be attained only by those who wait diligently upon God and who humbly submit their lives to His holy will.

Jesus, in all that He did, was supremely conscious of the approval of His heavenly Father. He was able to say, "I do always the things that are pleasing to him." And in response to His perfect obedience He heard again and again the voice of divine approval: "This is my beloved Son, in whom I am well pleased; hear ye him." This sense of oneness with the Father in thought and word and deed was the basis of our Lord's unfailing confidence, courage, peace and joy. He promised His joy and peace and courage to His immediate disciples and to all who would receive His words and walk in fellowship with Him. His Gospel, His example, His living presence in His Spirit assure all who seek to know and do His will that He is able to guide and keep and bless. Fear not, Christian; for thou hast found favor with God.

### III. To the Shepherds—The Courage of Assured Salvation.

Not in the Temple, not in a humble home, but out on the starlit hills of Bethlehem the angel of good tidings appeared to the shepherds. Jerusalem with its glorious Temple, Nazareth with its simple peasant home, Bethlehem with its sacred shepherd lore are all linked together by the angelic annunciations of Christmas. The angel that came by night to the shepherds in the fields said, "Be not afraid; for behold, I bring you good tidings of great joy which shall be to all the people: for there is born to you this day in the city of David a Saviour, who is Christ the Lord." The birth of the Saviour, the promised Messiah, is the central fact of Christmas. This message of assured salvation gave to the faithful shepherds a new spirit of courage, joy and hope for which they had been preparing and waiting. We cannot fail to wonder how it was that the shepherds and others who received the message from their lips could be so completely satisfied with just the good news of the Saviour's *birth*. They were as yet unacquainted with the full and complete revelation of the Son of God which unfolded with His public ministry, His atoning death, triumphant resurrection and glorious ascension. And yet the tidings of the Saviour's birth seemed to awaken in the hearts of the shepherds more of wonder, reverence, faith, joy and praise than the full Gospel of God's love in Christ Jesus arouses in the hearts of those who are less receptive and responsive to the joyous tidings of salvation. We are not inclined to pity the shepherds because they did not know as much as we know. Rather we are prone to pity ourselves that we cannot recapture the spirit of simple faith, reverent wonder, joyous praise, devout adoration, and radiant witnessing that was the spirit of the shepherds.

How many people go on from Christmas "glorifying and praising God for all the things they have heard and seen?" How many take with them into every day with its separate need the assurance that God will graciously and abundantly provide for their needs? How many courageously face the problems and trials of life with the confidence that victory and deliverance are assured by the grace of God? The message given to the shepherds tells us of the Saviour Who fully, completely and abundantly saves. He saves us from the guilt of sin by dying for us the death of the cross. He delivers us from the tyranny of sin by the sanctifying power of His indwelling Spirit. He saves His people from the tribulations, sorrows, and difficulties of life by giving them the strength, grace, and patience to bear them and use them for the glory of God. He saves society and nations and governments when men seek to build the Kingdom of righteousness, peace and good will. He saves all who are faithful unto death and brings them into the eternal Kingdom of the Father prepared from the foundation of the world. Let us learn anew the meaning of Christmas courage: the courage of answered prayer; the courage of divine approval; the courage of assured salvation. "Be of good courage; it is I; be not afraid."

*The Son of the Most High*

# ALL PRAISE TO THEE, ETERNAL LORD

*All praise to Thee, Eternal Lord,*
*Clothed in a garb of flesh and blood;*
*Choosing a manger for Thy throne,*
*While worlds on worlds are Thine alone.*

*Once did the skies before Thee bow;*
*A Virgin's arms contain Thee now:*
*Angels who did in Thee rejoice*
*Now listen for Thine infant voice.*

*A little Child, Thou art our Guest,*
*That weary ones in Thee may rest;*
*Forlorn and lowly is Thy birth,*
*That we may rise to heaven from earth.*

*Thou comest in the darksome night*
*To make us children of the light,*
*To make us, in the realms Divine,*
*Like Thine own angels round Thee shine.*

*All this for us Thy love hath done;*
*By this to Thee our love is won:*
*For this we tune our cheerful lays,*
*And shout our thanks in ceaseless praise.*

—MARTIN LUTHER, 1524.

# . VII

## THE SON OF THE MOST HIGH

LUKE 1:32-33, *He shall be great, and shall be called the Son of the Most High: and the Lord God shall give unto him the throne of his father David: and he shall reign over the house of Jacob for ever; and of his kingdom there shall be no end.*

FRA ANGELICO'S celebrated painting, "The Annunciation," is a work of delicate beauty and rare religious devotion. The sacred scene depicted by the Italian painter is thus described by Charles H. Caffin: "In the cool of the evening Mary has been surprised by God's messenger, Gabriel. He has but this moment alighted; his wings still glisten with the iridescence of the sky, and his body thrills yet with the rapidity of his flight, as he drops on one knee with bowed head and folded hands in adoration of her who is to be the mother of the Saviour. And at this apparition, flashing so suddenly across the quiet tenor of her days, Mary's face is troubled; but, as she harkens to the divine message, she too bows her head and folds her arms in adoration and in meek acceptance. 'And Mary said, Behold the handmaid of the Lord; be it unto me according to thy word'."

Luke's account of the Annunciation is characterized by the same spirit of beautiful simplicity, delicacy and reserve. How exquisitely beautiful are all of the annunciation scenes in Luke's Infancy Gospel! The angel Gabriel first appears to the priest Zacharias at the hour of prayer, beside the altar of incense, amidst the holy splendors of the Temple in Jerusalem. Then, Gabriel appears to the virgin Mary amidst the quiet seclusion of her humble home in Nazareth. And finally, the herald angel and the angelic choir appear to the watching shepherds in the starlit fields of Bethlehem. The keynote of all these scenes may well be: "Be still, and know that I am God."

Theodosia Garrison's poem, "The Annunciation," expresses something of the mystery and wonder of this event in the life of Mary.

> God whispered and a silence fell; the world
>   Poised one expectant moment like a soul
> Who sees at Heaven's threshold the unfurled
> White wings of cherubim, the sea impearled,
>   And pauses, dazed, to comprehend the whole;
> Only across all space God's whisper came
> And burned about her heart like some white flame.
>
> Then suddenly a bird's note thrilled the peace,
>   And earth again jarred noisily to life
> With a great murmur as of many seas.
> But Mary sat with hands clasped on her knees,
>   And lifted eyes with all amazement rife,
> And in her heart the rapture of the Spring
> Upon its first sweet day of blossoming.

The time, the place, the manner of Gabriel's appearance to Mary are all important. But the message the angel gave to Mary is of supreme importance. Hear again the amazing proclamation of God's messenger that fell upon the wondering ears of Mary: *"And behold, thou shalt conceive in thy womb, and bring forth a son, and shalt call his name JESUS. He shall be great, and shall be called the Son of the Most High: and the Lord God shall give unto him the throne of his father David: and he shall reign over the house of Jacob for ever; and of his kingdom there shall be no end."*

## I. His Name.

The name of a new-born child is always important. One of the first questions we ask concerning a child is, "What is his name?" The names given to Hebrew children were doubly important, as they were intended to indicate the nature and character of these children. In the case of Mary's son, the name was of the utmost significance. In general, the names and titles applied to Him describe His character and His mission.

In the New Testament generally, there are more than a hundred names, titles, and designations applied to Jesus. Taken together, they indicate His many-sided personality and His diversified mission. His is the name above every name, for He possessed in Himself the fulness of God and wrought out to completion in His earthly life the perfect will of God.

It is interesting and profitable to consider the names applied to Jesus in the Nativity narratives alone. In Matthew's Gospel, He is called *Jesus Christ, Jesus, Immanuel, King of the Jews, Governor, Shepherd, Son, Nazarene.* And in Luke's account, He is called *Jesus, Son of the Most High, Son of God, Saviour, Christ the Lord, the Lord's Christ.* He is also referred to as "the dayspring from on high" and "the consolation of Israel."

The names given to Mary's child describe His person, His nature, His character. They indicate His divine nature, His deity. He is the Son of God. That is, He shares the nature of God in a full and unique sense. He is like God His Father; He is all that God is; He is God. This is true not only of His essential nature, but it is true as to the manner of His Incarnation. He is the Son of the Most High; God is His Father; He is conceived by the Holy Spirit. The angel announced the mystery to Mary, saying, "The Holy Spirit shall come upon thee, and the power of the Most High shall overshadow thee: wherefore also the holy thing which is begotten shall be called the Son of God." In like manner, these names indicate His true humanity. The record speaks of "the *birth* of Jesus Christ." He was *born* of the virgin Mary. The fact that He was born of a human mother is sufficient evidence that He possessed human nature. John declares in his Prologue that He "became flesh, and dwelt among us." Paul states that He was "made in the likeness of men" and was "found in fashion as a man." He is the Son of man, as well as the Son of God. He is all that God is, and He is all that man is—the perfect God-Man.

The names given to the Christ also describe His mission
in the world. He came on a divinely-appointed mission. God
sent Him into the world. He is the Lord's Christ, the di-
vinely-anointed King. He is called JESUS, because He came
to save His people from their sins. JESUS is His real name,
His given name, His eternal name. He is the Saviour, Shepherd, and King. He came to save, to guide, to feed, to protect,
to keep His people. He is called the Lamb of God, because
He gave His life as a sacrifice to atone for the sins of the
world. He is God's Lamb, and He died to redeem mankind.
He came to be the Saviour of the whole world.

> "O the precious name of Jesus!
>   How it thrills our souls with joy,
> When His loving arms receive us,
>   And His songs our tongues employ!"

## II. His Throne.

Mary, the mother of Jesus, had royal blood in her veins.
She was of the house and lineage of David. She cherished the
hopes and promises God had given to His ancient people that
the Messiah would come from the house of David. She understood the message of Gabriel when he said concerning her
Son: "the Lord God shall give unto him the throne of his
father David." Why is David singled out as the chief ances-
tor of Christ? Why is he called the "father" of Christ? David was the founder of a dynasty of kings. He was divinely
chosen and anointed for this high office. He was the type
and precursor of Him Who was at the same time David's
Son and David's Lord. David was a prophet, shepherd, and
king. He was a man after God's own heart, and "did that
which was right in the eyes of the Lord, and turned not aside
from anything that he commanded him all the days of his life,
save only in the matter of Uriah the Hittite."

Mary's Son, then, was in a natural and typical sense the
Son of David. As Paul put it, He "was born of the seed of
David according to the flesh." He was the Son of David by
lineal descent, and in the sense of fulfilled prophecy that the
Messiah would come of the seed of David. In the highest pos-

sible sense, Jesus was divinely chosen and anointed as the King of Israel. He was the Lord's Christ, God's anointed King, "who was declared to be the Son of God with power, according to the spirit of holiness, by the resurrection from the dead." God gave Christ His throne.

Jesus laid claim to all of the rights and prerogatives of Deity. During His last week, when His enemies were trying to ensnare Him with difficult questions, He finally turned to them and asked them a question. To the Pharisees He said, "What think ye of the Christ? whose son is he?" They made answer, "The son of David." Then Christ said to them, "How then doth David in the Spirit call him Lord, saying,

> 'The Lord said unto my Lord,
> Sit thou on my right hand,
> Till I put thine enemies underneath thy feet?'

If David then calleth him Lord, how is he his son?" Thus Jesus insisted that He was more than the son of David after the flesh; that He was in truth the Son of God after the Spirit.

The important thing for us is that we give Christ His rightful place on the throne of our hearts and lives. He is the King of Kings and Lord of Lords according to God's own plan and decree. God has given Him the throne of universal power, dominion and glory. It is our privilege and obligation to enthrone Him over our wills and affections, our plans and purposes. "Who should be king save him who makes us free?" cried the youthful Gareth. It is that same "deathless King Who lived and died for men" Who declared, "If therefore the Son shall make you free, ye shall be free indeed." Lord, grant us the perfect freedom of lives wholly surrendered to Thy sovereign will.

## III. *His Reign.*

The greatness of the Son of the Most High is further declared in the angel's statement: "and he shall reign over the house of Jacob for ever." Again we are reminded of the roots of the Messiah in the deep past. His throne is the throne of His father David; His rule is over the house of Jacob. Jacob, one of the patriarchs, was the father of twelve sons after whom were named the twelve tribes of Israel. Jacob, the supplanter, was called Israel, a prince with God, after his experience of wrestling with the angel by the brook Jabbok. In time, the Hebrew nation came to be called "the Children of Israel." In the broad sense, then, "the house of Jacob" stands for all the people of God; for all who are spiritual descendants of Jacob; for all princely souls who love God whole-heartedly and submit themselves to His holy and beneficent will.

The Scriptures frequently speak of "the God of Jacob." The God of Jacob is the God Who is gracious, merciful, and forgiving. He is the God Who redeems, transforms, and delivers men. He changed Jacob from a mean, crafty, deceitful supplanter into a prince with God and with men. He touched the thigh of Jacob's selfish, sinful nature and caused it to wither and die. He enabled Jacob, through faith, to overcome the trials and temptations of life and to become a blessing to multitudes of the spiritual children of Israel.

The God of Jacob is the God and Father of our Lord Jesus Christ. In Christ, His redeeming love is made full and complete. Christ came to seek and to save the lost. He came to save sinners and to make them saints. He came to redeem, renew, re-create those who believe in Him. He changed the lives of all kinds of men and women in His own day and country. He has been doing this in all generations and in all lands for more than nineteen hundred years. "Jesus Christ is the same yesterday and today, yea and for ever." *He reigns over the house of Jacob*. He can exercise His rule only in the lives of those who know Him as Saviour and Lord. He rules those who have faith in Him. He rules those who have been delivered from their sins and who have been made new creatures in Christ Jesus. The spiritual sons of Jacob shall reign with Him for ever and ever.

## IV. *His Kingdom.*

"And of his kingdom there shall be no end." O the great-
ness of the Son of the Most High! His name, His throne,
His reign, His kingdom are eternal! This is true because the
King Himself is eternal. He is the Prince of life, the Lord of
glory, the resurrection and the life. He is the eternal Christ
Who said to the Seer of Patmos: "Fear not; I am the first
and the last, and the Living one; and I was dead, and behold,
I am alive for evermore, and I have the keys of death and of
Hades." He is the Christ of God, the only begotten Son of
the Father Whom Paul worshipped as "the blessed and only
Potentate, the King of kings, and Lord of lords; who only
hath immortality, dwelling in light unapproachable; whom
no man hath seen, nor can see: to whom be honor and power
eternal. Amen."

Then, Christ's Kingdom is endless because of the spiritual
nature and values of His Kingdom. It is the Kingdom of
God, the Kingdom of Heaven. It is the Kingdom of eternal
truth. It is the Kingdom of righteousness, peace, and joy in
the Holy Spirit. It is the Kingdom of love, mercy, and justice. The values of this spiritual realm are everlasting. "But
now abideth faith, hope, love, these three; and the greatest of
these is love." It is the "kingdom that cannot be shaken,"
though all of the kingdoms and empires of this world pass
away. It is related to the sovereign will of the eternal God,
and as such is not subject to the vicissitudes of temporal kingdoms. We are taught to pray: "Thy kingdom come. Thy
will be done." We are assured that "He that doeth the will
of God abideth for ever."

Men are deeply troubled and dismayed today because they
behold "the removing of those things that are shaken." It
is possible for us to give too much thought and attention to
this *changing* world. The kingdoms of this world are wicked-
ness, war, and sorrow in the spirit of evil. They have the
seeds of death and decay in them. "For all that is in the world,
the lust of the flesh and the lust of the eyes and the vain-
glory of life, is not of the Father, but is of the world. And

the world passeth away, and the lust thereof." All men need to think more of the everlasting love of the Father, of the unchanging Christ, and of the beneficent laws of His endless Kingdom. All men need to do precisely what the Son of the Most High has been patiently calling them to do: "But seek ye first his kingdom, and his righteousness; and all these things shall be added unto you." Those who faithfully seek His Kingdom find the supreme joy and blessedness of life. Those who belong to the King receive the free gift of God which is eternal life in Christ Jesus our Lord. In the spirit of humble faith and submission like unto that of Mary, the handmaid of the Lord, let us magnify the Lord and rejoice in God our Saviour, and let us exalt the name of JESUS, our eternal King.

> *"Crown Him with many crowns,*
> *The Lamb upon His throne;*
> *Hark! how the heavenly anthem drowns*
> *All music but its own:*
> *Awake, my soul, and sing*
> *Of Him who died for thee,*
> *And hail Him as thy matchless King*
> *Through all eternity."*

*The Spirit of Christmas*

## LOVE CAME DOWN AT CHRISTMAS

*Love came down at Christmas,*
  *Love all lovely, Love divine;*
*Love was born at Christmas,*
  *Stars and angels gave the sign.*

*Worship we the Godhead,*
  *Love incarnate, Love divine;*
*Worship we our Jesus:*
  *But wherewith for sacred sign?*

*Love shall be our token,*
  *Love be yours and love be mine,*
*Love to God and all men,*
  *Love for plea and gift and sign.*

—CHRISTINA ROSSETTI, (1830-1894).

# VIII

## THE SPIRIT OF CHRISTMAS

LUKE 1 :47, *And my spirit hath rejoiced in
God my Saviour.*

SHALL we ask, *What* is the Spirit of Christmas? or *Who*
is the Spirit of Christmas? Let us see. We know that the
Spirit of Christmas cannot be defined. It is intangible, mysterious, and incomprehensible. But it is real. It belongs not
to the seen things which are temporal, but to the unseen things
which are eternal. We can see the beneficent influences of its
power in the lives of men, women, and children, but we cannot tell whence it cometh or whither it goeth. It is like a
beam of light which can be passed through a prism and so re-
fracted as to form a beautiful spectrum of colors. So the
spectrum of the Christmas Spirit reflects the beauteous colors
of love, joy, peace, reverence, hope, charity and praise in
these lives of ours.

But the truly religious approach reveals that the real
Christmas Spirit is none other than the Holy Spirit Himself.
He is the Bringer of God's gift of His only begotten Son, and
the Inspirer of the songs and good tidings that make up the
Christmas message. The angel said to Mary, "The Holy
Spirit shall come upon thee, and the power of the Most High
shall overshadow thee: wherefore also the holy thing which
is begotten shall be called the Son of God." The record also
emphatically declares that Elisabeth, Mary, Zacharias, and
Simeon were filled with the Holy Spirit when they uttered
the songs of praise and blessing with which they greeted the
coming of the Messiah. The Holy Spirit, then, is the Author

and Inspirer of all the spiritual joys and good works that bless mankind with each return of the Christmas season.

## I. The Spirit of Hope.

The Spirit of Christmas is *the Spirit of Hope*. The hope of ancient Israel centered in the coming of the Messiah Who would bring redemption and peace to His people. This star of hope shone brightly down through the centuries, giving courage and patience to the faithful who waited upon God. The prophecy of Balaam the son of Beor is one of the most ancient and illuminating: "I shall see him, but not now: I shall behold him, but not nigh: there shall come a Star out of Jacob, and a Sceptre shall rise out of Israel" (Numbers 24:17). In the later centuries of Messianic prophecy the message of hope becomes more clear and distinct. Isaiah, the evangelistic prophet, declares: "The people that walked in darkness have seen a great light: they that dwelt in the land of the shadow of death, upon them hath the light shined" (Isaiah 9:2). And Micah clearly predicts the very birthplace of Messiah, saying, "But thou, Bethlehem, Ephrathah, which are little to be among the thousands of Judah, out of thee shall one come forth unto me that is to be ruler in Israel; whose goings forth are from of old, from everlasting" (Micah 5:2).

The spirit of longing expectancy was not confined entirely to the people of Israel; for the Wise-Men of the east, who were Gentiles, likewise cherished the hope of the dawning of a brighter day.

In the hearts of truly pious Israelites of Jesus' own day, notably Zacharias, Elisabeth, Joseph, Mary, Simeon, Anna and others, the hope of the coming Messiah burned and glowed like a star. To these quiet and devout souls the coming Messiah meant "help to Israel his servant", "a horn of salvation" to the house of David, "the consolation of Israel", "the redemption of Jerusalem", "A light for revelation to the Gentiles," and "the glory of thy people Israel." The birth of Jesus Christ marked the fulfilment of these age-long hopes, for He was the Messiah, the divinely anointed Christ and King. Hence, "the hopes and fears of all the years" are met in the birth of Jesus the Saviour.

## II. *The Spirit of Praise.*

The Spirit of Christmas is *the Spirit of Praise.* The songs of Zacharias, Elisabeth, Mary, and Simeon are songs of praise for Jehovah's salvation to His people. Their songs of praise were all inspired by the Spirit of God, and all glorify God as the Author of the manifold blessings that came to the world with the birth of the Son of the Most High. In like manner, the song of the angels heard by the wondering shepherds on the plains of Bethlehem was a song of praise and glory to God in the highest for His gift of love to mankind.

The Song of Elisabeth was the song of the mother of the "preparer" to the mother of Him for Whom he would prepare. It breathes the spirit of humility, reverence, and faith. It is filled with adoration and praise for the mother of "my Lord." Mary's song called the "Magnificat" is a lyrical meditation of pure praise to God for His mercy to His handmaid. Her hymn of praise dwells upon Jehovah's favor to her (the personal note) ; Jehovah's favor to the true seed of Abraham (the national note) ; Jehovah's favor to all humble ones (the universal note). The song of Zacharias called the "Benedictus" blesses God for the redemption of Israel through the Messiah, the Son of David.

As we sing the hymns of Christmas our hearts should be filled with the spirit of praise to God for His manifold blessings to us and to the world in the gift of His Son. We should seek to capture the spirit of pious devotion, humble submission, reverent adoration, and joyous exultation that filled the hearts of those who first welcomed Him with their songs.

## III. *The Spirit of Joy.*

The Spirit of Christmas is *the Spirit of Joy.* There is a deep undertone of joy running throughout the whole Christmas message. There are other notes, to be sure ; notes of sadness, sorrow, and suffering. But the predominant note, the all-pervasive note is one of profound spiritual joy. The Christmas Gospel anticipates and is in keeping with the message of Him Who said: "These things have I spoken unto you, that my joy may be in you, and that your joy may be made full" (John 15:11).

This Spirit of Joy is contained in the good tidings brought to the shepherds by the herald angel. "And the angel said unto them, Be not afraid; for behold, I bring you good tidings of *great joy* which shall be to all the people: for there is born to you this day in the city of David a Saviour, who is Christ the Lord." There was joy in the presence of the angels of heaven at the time of the Saviour's birth, and this heavenly joy was granted in fullest measure to the shepherds and to other human hearts prepared to receive it. The accomplished quest of the Wise-Men was in like manner an experience of joy and rejoicing for those kingly visitors from afar. The record reads, "And they, having heard the king, went their way; and lo, the star, which they saw in the east, went before them, till it came and stood over where the young child was. And when they saw the star, *they rejoiced with exceeding great joy.*" And what shall we say of the joy that came to Zacharias and Elisabeth when God gave them a son to cheer and comfort their old age and to fulfil a divinely appointed mission? And how shall we tell of the unspeakable joy that was known to Mary and Joseph as they received the holy charge God had given to them? And how shall we describe the perfect joy that crowned the closing days of those devout saints, Simeon and Anna, as their longing hearts were cheered and comforted by the sight of the Infant Saviour?

Surely our Christmas joy should be "made full" as we think of the full revelation of the Gospel of God's grace and truth that we possess. The faithful souls who received the Christ Child saw only the dawning light of "the dayspring from on high." But we dwell in the bright noon-day of the Sun of Righteousness, fully risen with healing in His wings. Hence it should be out of hearts that are filled with "the joy of the Lord" that we sing the Christmas message:

*"Joy to the world! the Lord is come:*
*Let earth receive her King."*

## IV. *The Spirit of Adoration.*

The Spirit of Christmas is *the Spirit of Adoration.* The shepherds, the saints, and the Wise-Men adored and worshipped the Christ Child in deed and in truth. The shepherds had the most unique and precious experience of all. They came and found both Mary and Joseph, and the babe lying in the manger. They were prepared in heart and spirit by the message of the angels to worship most humbly and devoutly at this strange altar: the manger where a new-born babe wrapped in swaddling clothes was lying! The saints, Simeon and Anna, were in their accustomed place of worship, the Temple in Jerusalem, when Mary and Joseph came in to present their six weeks old child to the Lord. They were prepared by many long years of unceasing prayer and longing expectancy to receive the Lord's Christ. They were inspired by the Spirit of God to adore and worship Mary's Child with grateful, loving hearts and with revealing utterances of prophetic truth. The Wise-Men sometime later found Mary and the Christ Child in a house in Bethlehem, and there they fell down and worshipped Him and offered their princely gifts to Him. The mother's adoration of her Saviour Child is reflected in her song and is still more beautifully suggested in the words, "But Mary kept all these sayings, pondering them in her heart."

These to whom Christ first came worshipped Him in the starlit fields, the lowly stable, the magnificent Temple, the humble home, the loving heart. The *place* of worship is important, to be sure. But wherever we are, we can worship Him acceptably only as our hearts are filled with love, adoration, and trust. We must worship Him not only as a sweet and innocent Child, but as Immanuel—God with us. We must worship Him as Jesus the Saviour, Christ the Lord. We must worship Him in word and deed and life. Our worship is complete only when we surrender ourselves to Him and devote the spiritual and material treasures of our lives to His Kingdom that shall have no end.

## V. *The Spirit of Giving.*

The Spirit of Christmas is *the Spirit of Giving.* The one example in the Christmas story of the giving of material gifts is that of the Wise-Men who presented gold, frankincense and myrrh to the Christ Child. But in a larger and truer sense, Christmas *is* essentially giving. Christmas stands for God's gift of love to mankind. "For God so loved the world, that he gave his only begotten Son, that whosoever believeth on him should not perish, but have eternal life." Someone has given us a remarkable interpretation of the meaning of God's Gift of Love in the following lines:

> *God—the greatest LOVER.*
> *So loved—the greatest DEGREE.*
> *The world—the greatest COMPANY.*
> *That He gave—the greatest ACT.*
> *His only begotten Son—the greatest GIFT.*
> *That whosoever—the greatest OPPORTUNITY.*
> *Believeth—the greatest SIMPLICITY.*
> *In Him—the greatest ATTRACTION.*
> *Should not perish—the greatest PROMISE.*
> *But—the greatest DIFFERENCE.*
> *Have—the greatest CERTAINTY.*
> *Eternal life—the greatest POSSESSION.*

God gave His Son to die for us on the cross and to redeem us from our sins. Paul was thinking of this when he wrote to the Romans, "He that spared not his own Son, but delivered him up for us all, how shall he not also with him freely give us all things?" Again Paul suggests the exceeding preciousness of God's gift in his words to the Corinthians: "For ye know the grace of our Lord Jesus Christ, that, though he was rich, yet for your sakes he became poor, that ye through his poverty might become rich."

We express the spirit of true Christmas giving when we give in love and in the spirit of sacrificial service.

## VI. *The Spirit of Peace.*

The Spirit of Christmas is *the Spirit of Peace.* The voice of Hebrew prophecy acclaimed the coming Messiah as the Prince of Peace. Isaiah sounds this Gospel note: "For unto us a child is born, unto us a son is given; and the government shall be upon his shoulder: and his name shall be called Wonderful, Counsellor, Mighty God, Everlasting Father, Prince of Peace" (Isaiah 9:6). The prophet Micah gives us this winsome picture: "And he shall stand, and shall feed his flock in the strength of Jehovah, in the majesty of the name of Jehovah his God: and they shall abide; for now shall he be great unto the ends of the earth. And this man shall be our peace" (Micah 5:4-5a).

Zacharias, the father of the Forerunner, declared that the coming of the Messiah would bring the blessing of peace to Israel.

> *"Whereby the dayspring from on high shall visit us,*
> *To shine upon them that sit in darkness and the shadow of death;*
> *To guide our feet into the way of peace."*

This was the promise given to the shepherds as they heard the angel choir praising God, and saying,

> *"Glory to God in the highest,*
> *And on earth peace among men in whom he is well pleased."*

This was the personal message of fulfilment and salvation that came to devout Simeon as he held the Infant Saviour in his arms.

> *"Now lettest thou thy servant depart, O Lord,*
> *According to thy word, in peace;*
> *For mine eyes have seen thy salvation."*

The gift of the Prince of Peace to those who truly abide in Him is peace with God, peace with one's fellowmen, peace with the world, peace within the heart. It was this Prince of Peace Who later said to His disciples: "Peace I leave with you; my peace I give unto you: not as the world giveth, give I unto you. Let not your heart be troubled, neither let it be fearful." "These things have I spoken unto you, that in me ye may have peace."

## VII. *The Spirit of Love.*

The Spirit of Christmas is *the Spirit of Love.* God the Father has shown His gracious and forgiving love in the gift of His well beloved Son. Paul says, "But God commendeth his own love toward us, in that, while we were yet sinners,

Christ died for us." John affirms, "Herein is love, not that we loved God, but that he loved us, and sent his Son to b the propitiation for our sins." Jesus declared this love of th Father for His children in word and deed and life. In Hi intercessory prayer on behalf of all believers, He says to th Father, "thou didst send me, and *lovedst them, even as thou lovedst me.*" He says further, "for thou lovedst me befor the foundation of the world," and concludes His prayer witl the petition "that the love wherewith thou lovedst me ma; be in them, and I in them." God is love. God gives Himsel in the gift of His Son. Those who receive the Son have th love of God shed abroad in their hearts.

Christ has shown His sacrificial and redeeming love fo His own in that He died the death of the cross. His word are, "Greater love hath no man than this, that a man la; down his life for his friends."

The loving Saviour and Lord has commanded His disciple; and friends to show this love to one another. "A new com mandment I give unto you, that ye love one another; even a; I have loved you, that ye also love one another. By this shal all men know that ye are my disciples, if ye have love one to another." "But I say unto you that hear, Love your enemies do good to them that hate you, bless them that curse you, pra; for them that despitefully use you."

The Spirit of Christmas which is the Spirit of Hope Praise, Joy, Adoration, Giving, Peace, and Love is the free gift of God in Christ Jesus our Lord and is the abiding pos session of those who walk in the Holy Spirit.

*Song of Good Will*

# HARK! WHAT MEAN THOSE HOLY VOICES

Hark! what mean those holy voices,
  Sweetly warbling in the skies?
Sure the angelic host rejoices,
  Loudest Alleluias rise.

Listen to the wondrous story,
  Which they chant in hymns of joy:
"Glory in the highest, glory;
  Glory be to God Most High!

"Peace on earth, good-will from heaven,
  Reaching far as man is found;
Souls redeemed, and sins forgiven;
  Loud our golden harps shall sound.

"Christ is born, the great Anointed;
  Heaven and earth His glory sing:
Glad receive whom God appointed
  For your Prophet, Priest, and King.

"Hasten, mortals, to adore Him;
  Learn His Name, and taste His joy;
Till in heaven you sing before Him,
  Glory be to God Most High!"

Let us learn the wondrous story
  Of our great Redeemer's birth,
Spread the brightness of His glory,
  Till it cover all the earth.

—Rev. John Cawood, 1819.

# IX

## SONG OF GOOD WILL

LUKE 2:14, *Glory to God in the highest, and on earth peace, good will toward men.*

THE Christmas Season is preeminently the season of good will among men. The divine music made by the Angel Chorus over the hills of Bethlehem is still re-echoing down the years. The rapturous strains heard by the wondering shepherds have never entirely died out. To the listening ear, those heavenly cadences, far from dying out in the distance, appear to be increasing in volume and harmony, until the whole world is filled with the ravishing melody.

This is the wonder of Christmas, that it brings with each passing year a re-birth of the spirit of friendliness, generosity and good will. There are many legends about the new life that comes into Nature with the approach of Christmas. It is said that the holly and the ivy are full grown; that the thorn-tree breaks forth into blossom; that the animals are endued with the power of speech. These legends of Nature are in keeping with what we know to be the facts concerning our human nature, namely, that there are new infusions of spiritual qualities which manifest themselves in many beautiful ways.

There is something about Christmas that rebukes the sordidness, the selfishness, the sinfulness of our natures; something that purges away the harshness, the callousness, the surliness of our habitual manner. As we draw nigh the sacred scene of the manger at Bethlehem — a scene we had almost forgotten during the rush and preoccupation of the past months — we are transformed into adoring, wondering worshippers as were the shepherds and Wise Men of old.

93

Then gradually or precipitately, as the case may be, something begins to happen in our hearts. A softening, a mellowing, a warming occurs—like the lighting of a blazing fire in a cold and cheerless room. The old feelings come back; memories revive that link the present with all of the years that are past and gone; memories of Christmas joy and happiness when we were children.

And we begin to feel differently toward others. There steals into our hearts a feeling of good will toward all men; a feeling of pity for the poor and needy; a wave of sympathy that leads us to do kind and helpful things for them. And so all over this world of ours, the Christmas Season works its magic spell. It brings a note of joy into the sadness of the world; a note of consolation into the sorrow of the world. The "still, sad music of humanity" is for a time drowned out by the triumphant music of "joy to the world!" This Spirit of Christmas brings a fresh infusion of neighborliness, kindness, peace and good will. It causes us to cease from our labors, to forget our anxieties and to listen for a little while to the song of the angels proclaiming glory to God in the highest, and on earth peace, good will among men.

### I. The Broadening of Good Will.

Let this spirit of peace and good will be extended and deepened and applied to all of our human relationships! Let it possess our hearts not only during the Christmas season, but from one Christmas to the next! Let it pervade our hearts and homes, our churches and communities, our nation and the nations of the world! Let it be felt in our industrial, political, social and religious life; let it become the watchword of all people everywhere! That is what Christmas is intended to be, a time when men shall consider the will of God the Father and the obligation to treat all men as brothers.

We cannot consider the ideal that Christmas holds before us without realizing our shortcomings in this regard. Christmas would not be touching us with its message unless it produced in us a feeling of penitence for our failure to cherish good will toward those around us.

How is it with us as regards the family circle? Do we have a feeling of good will toward all the members of our own family? Good will, like charity, should begin at home. Have we been guilty during the past year of breaking this bond of good will by speaking unkind words, by being thoughtless, inconsiderate and selfish? Have we caused heartache to those who are nearest to us by not showing the sympathy, love and understanding for one another that we ought? If we have been guilty of these failures for an hour, for a day, or for long, dreary months, let us set things right by opening once more the fountain of good will toward all of our dear ones. Let us cleanse the buried wells, as Isaac digged again the wells of his father Abraham, so that the life-giving waters may flow again. For how can we enter fully into the Spirit of Christmas unless we contribute to the happiness and well being of those who are nearest to us?

Then what about the church circle? Do we have a feeling of good will toward all of the members of our church? If not, why not? Is it possible for genuine Christians to hold ill will against their fellow Christians? We pray to God, "Forgive us our debts as we forgive our debtors." Now if God's forgiveness of our debts is conditioned by our forgiveness of others, what kind of forgiveness have we of God? John writes in his First Epistle, "Beloved, let us love one another: for love is of God; and every one that loveth is begotten of God, and knoweth God." And again, "If any man say, I love God, and hateth his brother, he is a liar: for he that loveth not his brother whom he hath seen, cannot love God whom he hath not seen." Unless every Christian has a feeling of good will toward every other Christian there is something wrong. For when Christ fills the believer's heart, there is no room for positive ill will toward any fellow Christian.

Surely Christmas is the season for the birth of the spirit of general good will among all people. Let us forget our old animosities, our petty grievances, our narrow prejudices. Let us make an end of thinking unkind thoughts about our fellow Christians, of speaking unkind words about them, of doing mean things to vex or displease them. Let us rather open all of the windows of our souls to receive the fresh and sweet currents of good will that are stirring at the Christmas Season. Only as we do this can we have a true fellowship of believers; a Church that is pure, peaceable and Christ-like; a brotherhood that furnishes the right example to the world.

Let us extend this spirit of good will to all peoples, in our communities, in our nation and in the world. Let us cultivate the feeling of good will toward those whom we class as foreigners in our communities, and toward those of different religious beliefs. Let us apply this panacea to the racial problems that are so acute even in our democratic country. Let us cherish the Christian spirit of good will toward the negroes, the Orientals, and the immigrants from the continent of Europe. We are not thinking merely of a shallow and superficial sentiment of mild tolerance toward these peoples. We are thinking rather of the spirit of Christian good will, deep and permanent, that expresses itself in life and conduct, and in our actual treatment of these races. Certainly the good will which constituted the theme of the angels' song was not a narrow or provincial or racial thing. It was universal in its scope and applied to all races, colors and classes of men.

## II. *The Deep-Lying Springs of Good Will.*

In order to make the Spirit of Christmas regnant in our lives the year round, we must know something about the deeplying springs of good will. We make a sad mistake if we suppose that the spirit of good will may be easily obtained and kept. This spirit is not a genie that we can summon at will and employ for our uses. Rather it is a flower that grows in the soil of the human heart only when that soil is prepared by the influences of the true religion of Jesus Christ. When the angels sang of peace on earth, "good will toward men", they also sang of "Glory to God in the highest." That is where good will begins, in ascribing glory to God the Father. The human heart engaged in worshipful adoration of Almighty God is at once possessed with the spirit of peace and good will toward men. The shepherds and the Wise Men found a new spirit of peace, joy and good will in praising and glorifying God, and in worshiping the Christ Child whose name was Immanuel, God with us.

Our lives will radiate the spirit of good will toward all men only as we reverence and worship the Son of God and faithfully follow in His footsteps. Good will that is perpetual and deep and lasting is a work of God's grace in our hearts. We cannot cherish good will as an unfailing stream toward those around us by our own power. We need God's help to do this; we need the life of Christ within us. We are too selfish, too easily irritated, too revengeful to be always kindly and charitable and forgiving toward others. That is true of our human nature. But if we live in Christ and if He lives in us, then the things that are impossible to our human nature are possible to our divine nature. That is why God sent His only begotten Son into the world, that we might not perish in our sins and failures, but that by believing in Him we might have eternal life and the ability to do His holy will.

We can be kind and loving to those nearest and dearest to us if we rely upon Christ for grace and strength. We can be charitable and forgiving toward our brethren in the Lord if we are filled with the Spirit of Him Who said, "Love one another; even as I have loved you." We can go farther than this and, by His grace, keep this other commandment, "Love your enemies, and pray for them that despitefully use you, and persecute you." We can surmount our prejudices toward other races if we remember that He Who died for all men desires us to regard all men as brothers. The Spirit of Christ is the source of good will in human hearts. If we drink of that Spirit, the fountain of good will becomes in us a well of water springing up perpetually and flowing out into the lives of all men producing gladness, joy and peace.

## III. *The Fruits and Blessings of Good Will.*

The fruits and blessings of this general spirit of good will are manifold. Joy and happiness, kindness and sympathy, sincerity and friendship, service and sacrifice — all of these blessings abound where good will reigns. What a boon

Christmas is to the world in causing these blessings to abound among all men of good will!

Let us note what Christmas does each year in stimulating sympathy for the poor and needy and helpless. Millions of dollars are devoted to works of charity and mercy. Thousands of workers are enlisted in the cause of making Christmas bright and cheerful for the children of the poor. Christmas is indeed a God-send for the destitute and unfortunate. They receive many kindnesses and blessings which are unknown to them the rest of the year. Most of our great cities raise community funds amounting to thousands of dollars which are spent in trying to make Christmas real to the hungry, the naked, the sick and the lonely. God bless all of these agencies and all individuals who are trying to interpret the love and sympathy of the compassionate Christ to the needy and distressed. We remember that our Lord said, "Inasmuch as ye have done it unto one of the least of these my brethren, ye have done it unto me." Here is the marvel, that we are not only making Christmas happy for these little ones, but we are making Christmas happy for our Saviour too!

Let us also note the spiritual gains that accrue to all cheerful givers at Christmas time. The givers are blessed as well as the receivers. Many hearts that are hard and cold and selfish are thawed out and melted and warmed around the Christmas hearth. You remember what happened to old Scrooge in Dicken's Christmas Carol, how he found that the only way to happiness lay in doing good to the poor and needy. Thus Christmas impresses upon our hearts the old, old story that it is more blessed to give than to receive.

Once again, Christmas with its high tide of unselfishness and good will reveals to us the spiritual possibilities of the race. It shows us the high plane upon which we may and ought to live all the time. It shows us how much better people become when they truly consider Jesus Christ and worship Him in the beauty of holiness. Kneeling around the cradle of Bethlehem, men discover what God is like and what God can do in the life of man through His blessed Son.

God be praised that He has spoken to us in language that all can understand; in language that appeals to the depths of our human nature. God be praised that He sent His Son "a little baby thing" whom all can love and worship and adore. God be praised that all of us in this far off day who kneel in reverence before the holy Child wrapped in swaddling clothes and lying in a manger can, if we will but listen, hear once more the angels sing: "Glory to God in the highest, and on earth peace, good will toward men."

> *"Glory to God!" the lofty strain*
> *The realm of ether fills;*
> *How sweeps the song of solemn joy*
> *O'er Judah's sacred hills!*
> *"Glory to God!" the sounding skies*
> *Loud with their anthems ring:*
> *"Peace on the earth; good-will to men,*
> *From heaven's eternal King."*

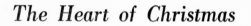

*The Heart of Christmas*

## O ONE WITH GOD THE FATHER

*O one with God the Father*
  *In majesty and might,*
*The Brightness of His glory,*
  *Eternal Light of light,*
*O'er this our home of darkness*
  *Thy rays are streaming now;*
*The shadows flee before Thee;*
  *The world's true Light art Thou.*

*Yet, Lord, we see but darkly;*
  *O heavenly Light, arise,*
*Dispel these mists that shroud us,*
  *And hide Thee from our eyes!*
*We long to track the footprints*
  *That Thou Thyself hast trod;*
*We long to see the pathway*
  *That leads to Thee, our God.*

*O Jesus, shine around us*
  *With radiance of Thy grace;*
*O Jesus, turn upon us*
  *The brightness of Thy face.*
*We need no star to guide us,*
  *As on our way we press,*
*If Thou Thy light vouchsafest,*
  *O Sun of Righteousness.*

—WILLIAM WALSHAM HOW, 1871.

# X

## THE HEART OF CHRISTMAS

JOHN 3:16, *For God so loved the world, that he gave his only begotten Son, that whosoever believeth on him should not perish, but have eternal life.*

THE opening stanza of Phillips Brooks' beautiful "Christmas Carol" contains the lines:

> *"The heart of the jewel burns lustrous and fair,*
> *And its soul full of music breaks forth on the air,*
> *When the song of the angels is sung."*

It is our desire to look into "the heart of the jewel" of Christmas and to share some of the beautiful things we see there.

### I. *At the Heart of Christmas—A Baby.*

First of all, there is at the heart of Christmas a baby. This baby is not different in appearance from other normal and healthy small babies. Of course the mother thinks He is the only baby boy in all the world, and to her He is more beautiful than any child she has ever seen. The baby that the shepherds see is a tiny little bundle wrapped in swaddling clothes and lying in a manger of clean straw. The baby is asleep, and the shepherds walk softly and speak with hushed voices for fear of waking Him. They take a peep at the slumbering Infant as Mary gently uncovers His little round face, and with the wonderful words the angels had spoken to them fresh in their minds the shepherds think He is an adorable child and as beautiful as a new-born baby may be.

The little baby the devout old Simeon takes in his arms in the temple is six weeks old. The baby weighs between ten and eleven pounds now, and looks up with wide-open eyes at the strange man. It is an absorbing picture: this venerable man holding in his frail arms the Salvation of the world and mumbling strange words concerning the innocent child and the perplexed mother. The old man is happier than a grandfather, for to him the child is not an ordinary child; He is the Lord's Christ, the promised Consolation of Israel.

The happy, interesting, joyous, never-to-be-forgotten days of babyhood are over when the Wise-men come to Bethlehem to worship the Christ Child. Only the mother's heart is filled with the treasured memories of cooing and smiling, of pink fingers clutching pink toes, of baby's first tooth, of the first tottering steps, and of a hundred other precious and tender memories of the months that have passed all too quickly. The Wise-men see a fine little boy nearly two years old, bright-eyed, sturdy and strong, and quick to answer their questions as to His name and age and other things. The Wise-men feel well repaid for their long journey, as the beautiful child gives them a happy smile and a gracious "Thank you" for the bright presents they give to Him.

Is it not strange and wonderful that a little baby is at the center of Christmas? If we understand why this should be so, then we know a great deal about the wisdom and love of God, and about God's plan for human life.

It is true that a few pure and loving hearts knew that the Messiah would be born as a little babe. Mary knew it, and Joseph knew it, after the angel of the Lord had made it known to them. Isaiah had uttered numerous prophecies concerning the Messiah-child many centuries before His birth. Said he, "A virgin shall conceive, and bear a son, and shall call his name Immanuel." Again, "For unto us a child is born, unto us a son is given." And again, "A little child shall lead them." Simeon and Anna understood the truth of these prophecies, and recognized their fulfillment in the child of Mary and Joseph. But the Hebrew nation as a whole did not look for the fulfillment of their hopes in the offspring of a

lowly peasant mother. George MacDonald's lines describe
the common belief:

> *"They all were looking for a king*
> *To slay their foes and lift them high:*
> *Thou cam'st, a little baby thing*
> *That made a woman cry."*

It is conceivable that the Son of Man could have come with
clouds of glory, as some thought He would come. It is conceivable that He might have appeared in all of His divine
majesty and sovereign power, even as the goddess Athena
was said to have sprung full-grown and full-armed from the
head of Zeus. But He did not choose to come in any such manner. Rather He came as "a little baby thing," helpless, innocent, and lovable.

The manner of His coming is more to be wondered at than
explained. But this we do know, that God loves and hallows
everything that is represented in the Nativity of His Son.
God loves a little baby. He is our heavenly Father. With
true Fatherly love He cherishes the precious life, and bestows
upon the helpless little one His tenderest solicitude and care.
There is no need to ask any question about the love of God
when we find love so full in our own natures. The explana-
tion of our love for our children is this: "We love because he
first loved us." Our love is but a dim reflection of God's perfect love for His children.

God honors and exalts parenthood. Marriage is sacred,
motherhood is sacred, childhood is sacred, the home is sacred
in the light of the radiance that shines from the Bethlehem
cradle. There are far too many people in this crass and sor-
did world who have lost this radiance, and who need to find it
again in the scene which the shepherds beheld.

God chooses to accomplish His purposes in the world
through human channels. Father, mother, and child constitute a holy trinity used of God and blessed of God in the accomplishment of His will on earth. Jesus, the true Son of
Man and the true Son of God, accomplished this purpose in a
superlative degree. But every son of man is intended to glori-

fy God by the doing of His will on earth as it is done in heaven.

God loves the qualities in human life represented in the Nativity of His Son. God sets His seal of approval upon the simplicity, the lowliness, the humility that marked His coming into the world. This is something for vainglorious people to think about. God does not care for all the pomp, splendor, pride, wealth, and vanity of human life. These things where regnant in the world are not according to His will. God gave His Son for the salvation of the world to poor, humble, devout, loving people. His highest glory was revealed in the humblest things of life. There are countless people in the world to-day who think themselves too poor and too lowly to be of any service to God. On the other hand, there are many people who think they are achieving the highest success in life if they amass great fortunes, or win the applause of men, or wield the sceptre of power over their fellows. The manger scene tells us that the very poorest may be rich if they love God and live close to Him; it tells us likewise that those who are the richest in this world's goods are poor indeed apart from God's love and blessing. When God shows us so clearly what He wants and approves in human life—as He does show us in the Nativity of His Son—it is utter folly for us to seek those things that do not fit in with the pattern of simplicity, humility, and love that is set before us.

The baby at the heart of Christmas is unmistakably a part of the life of God. The child Jesus was conceived of the Holy Spirit. His little life came into the world direct from God. He came from the Father into the world, and after His work was finished, He went back to the Father in heaven. If we are not too blind to see it, we will learn from this that every baby born into the world is a part of the divine life—a gift from God. This truth has been well stated by Tennyson in his poem "De Profundis", written on the birth of the poet's eldest son.

> "Out of the deep, my child, out of the deep,
> From that great deep, before our world begins,
> Whereon the Spirit of God moves as he will—
> Out of the deep, my child, out of the deep,

*From that true world within the world we see,*
*Whereof our world is but the bounding shore—*
*Out of the deep, Spirit, out of the deep,*
*With this ninth moon, that sends the hidden sun*
*Down yon dark sea, thou comest, darling boy."*

Our modern age pretends to know all about children; all about their bodies; all about their minds, and so on and so on. But we have forgotten one important fact, namely, that a child has a soul. We have forgotten that a child is a gift of God, a part of the life of God, born into the world to do the will of God, and to be taught above all else the love of God in Jesus Christ, so that at the last his soul may return to God Who gave it redeemed and glorified by the saving power of Jesus Christ.

## II. *At the Heart of Christmas—A Loving Heavenly Father.*

At the heart of Christmas there is a loving heavenly Father. The heart of the Gospel tells us that. "For God so loved the world, that he gave his only begotten Son, that whosoever believeth on him should not perish, but have eternal life." Jesus is the supreme gift of God's love to the world. Jesus reveals that at the center of this universe there is the heavenly Father's heart of love. After He came, men could say, "God is love." They could not say this before He came. Holiness and justice were the essential attributes of the God of the Old Testament. The other religions of the ancient world were infinitely farther from the conception of a loving God than the Hebrew religion. The religions of the world to-day do not know God as a God of love. The Mohammedan conception of God is utterly devoid of the attribute of love. Christianity tells us that God is love. Jesus revealed God's love by His teachings, His ministry, His character, and preeminently by His saving death on the cross. The highest expression of love that the world has seen is in the cross of Christ where God Himself suffers and gives His life for the sins of the world.

Our heavenly Father's love is a giving, sacrificing love. He so loved that He gave His only begotten Son. From this Paul reasons that God will give to His children everything else that they need. "He that spared not his own Son, but delivered him up for us all, how shall he not also with him freely give us all things?" "My God shall supply every need of yours according to his riches in glory in Christ Jesus."

The love of our heavenly Father is a forgiving love. Jesus published abroad this forgiving love when He forgave the sins of the penitent people who came to Him. He told the Parable of the Prodigal Son to set forth the yearning, forgiving, restoring love of God the Father toward all of His returning children.

The love of our Father in heaven is a keeping love. There is nothing in the power of life or death, in this world or the next that can separate us from the love of God in Christ Jesus. The love of God is immeasurable. Its length and breadth and depth cannot be fathomed or known completely. We can know enough for our eternal salvation and fulness of joy, and that is all we need to know. We know God's Fatherly love because He chose to send His beloved Son as His Christmas gift to the world.

### III. *At the Heart of Christmas—A Saviour.*

Once more, there is at the heart of Christmas a Saviour. This is the supreme fact that makes the Christmas message one of glad tidings of great joy for all people. God's angel said to Joseph, "Thou shalt call his name JESUS; for it is he that shall save his people from their sins." The angel said to the shepherds, "there is born to you this day in the city of David a Saviour, who is Christ the Lord."

Israel had produced many leaders that were wise and good, great and powerful. Priests and prophets, warriors and kings, poets and teachers, law-givers and reformers were included among Israel's great men and women. Israel had the law, the covenant, the promises and the correct ritual for the worship of God. But with all these things, God-given as they were, Israel could not meet the needs of the world. Israel's greatest prophets were always looking for Him Who should come to accomplish what the nation could not accomplish. God's purposes for the spiritual deliverance of His people were not to be fulfilled by law-givers, priests, warriors, kings, or prophets. If so, then Moses, Aaron, Joshua, David, or Elijah would have met the need. In the economy of God all of these were but types of Him Who was yet to come. These all looked for and relied upon the promises of a Saviour. These all needed God's perfect Prophet, Priest, and King Who could save them from their sins by His atoning death. This is the reason we see Moses and Elijah on the Mount of Transfiguration talking with Jesus about His coming death at Jerusalem. They expected something from His death for themselves and for all of God's people. The glory and the hope and the longings of Israel through the centuries were met and fulfilled in the coming of Jesus, the Messiah and Saviour.

Man's greatest need is for this Saviour. Man's life is from God. He is made in God's image. But his life has been marred by sin, so that he is a guilty creature in God's sight. Furthermore, by reason of the law of sin in man's nature he is not able to do what he ought to do. All power and inspiration for the achievement of the highest good in life come from God. If man is to receive this power and inspiration he must be in right relationship with God.

Man does not inherit this right relationship by birth, however godly his parents may have been. It is not the result of environment, however wholesome that may be. It does not lie in the power of his own will. Education alone cannot give him what he needs. Money cannot buy it. It is not in the power of government to confer it upon him. Even the Church, so far as its external organization is concerned, cannot supply his need. There is only One Who can meet man's deepest need. He is Jesus the Saviour. He alone can forgive man's sin, reconcile man with God, give him a new heart, and supply him with the Holy Spirit Who gives power, inspiration, guidance, comfort, truth, hope, patience and love and satisfies the spiritual cravings of man's soul. This Saviour came into the world on that first Christmas of the long ago. He came as a little babe, wrapped in swaddling clothes, and lying in a manger. In all that we know of Him in His after life, He declared the loving Fatherhood of God, and by His death upon the cross He openly offered Himself as the Saviour of the world. He rose from the dead on the third day, and forty days later He ascended into heaven. He is alive for evermore, and He dwells with His people through His Holy Spirit, Who imparts unto them the fulness of God. He is present in the hearts of all true believers. He is the Heart of Christmas, the Son of Man, the Lord of Glory, the Redeemer of the world.

## Part Three

# Christmas Treasures

# SILENT NIGHT! HOLY NIGHT!

*Silent night! Holy night!*
  *All is dark, save the light*
*Yonder, where they sweet vigils keep,*
  *O'er the Babe who in silent sleep,*
    *Rests in heavenly peace,*
    *Rests in heavenly peace.*

*Silent night! Peaceful night!*
  *Darkness flies, all is light;*
*Shepherds hear the angels sing,*
  *"Alleluia! hail the King!*
    *Christ the Saviour is born,*
    *Jesus the Saviour is born."*

*Silent night! Holy night!*
  *Child of heaven, O how bright*
*Was Thy smile when Thou wast born!*
  *Blest indeed that happy morn,*
    *Full of heavenly joy,*
    *Full of heavenly joy!*

*Silent night! Holy night!*
  *Guiding star, lend thy light!*
*See the Eastern Wise Men bring*
  *Gifts and homage to our King!*
    *Christ the Saviour is born,*
    *Jesus the Saviour is born!*

*Silent night! Holiest night!*
  *Wondrous star, lend thy light!*
*With the angels let us sing*
  *Alleluia to our King!*
    *Christ the Saviour is born,*
    *Jesus the Saviour is born!*

—Rev. Joseph Mohr, 1818.

## XI

## CHRISTMAS TREASURES

MATTHEW 2:11, *And they came into the house and saw the young child with Mary his mother; and they fell down and worshipped him; and opening their treasures they offered unto him gifts, gold and frankincense and myrrh.*

THE epochal journey and the life-long quest of the Wise-Men from the east came to an end in a humble home of Bethlehem where they found a young mother and her first-born child. Two things the Wise-Men did at that historic moment: they fell down and worshipped the Child, and offered precious gifts to Him. The Child was too young to understand the meaning of it all, but Heaven understood and possibly the mother understood. We think we understand, but our world in general is far, far away from imitating the worship and homage of the Wise-Men.

When we come to ourselves, we know that the Wise-Men did the right thing in worshipping the Christ Child and in offering their most precious gifts to Him. We know that the acceptance of the Kingship of Christ inevitably involves the dedication of life's treasures to Him. The Wise-Men opened their *treasures,* the most valuable things they possessed, and offered them in the spirit of adoration and worship to Christ, the new-born King.

Down through the years a great host of worshipful and consecrated servants of the King have followed in the train of the Wise-Men and have laid their most precious treasures at His feet. These offerings are the best that the human mind and heart and spirit have brought forth. They constitute the real treasures of Christmas on the human side—the treasures that have been brought to Christ by His servants. We do not now speak of the treasures Christ has brought to the world. Let us think about some of these treasures of the human spirit that belong especially to the Christ Child. They are, indeed, spiritual gifts of gold and frankincense and myrrh.

1. *The Treasures of Hymns.* Phillips Brooks has given a precious gift to the Saviour in his Christmas Carol, "O Little Town of Bethlehem." Concerning the origin of this hymn we are told that during Christmas week of 1865 the author rode on horseback from Jerusalem to Bethlehem, and that the view of this little town set on the eastern slope of a Judean hill, with terraced vineyards about it, inspired the writing of this hymn. The abiding message of the hymn lies in the suggestion that as Christ was born in Bethlehem centuries ago in the silent watches of the night, so in silence He comes today and is born anew in the hearts of those who will receive Him. We cannot tell how many hearts have been opened to receive "the dear Christ" by the sweet influence of this treasured hymn.

There is the treasure laid at His feet by Joseph Mohr, author of the hymn, "Silent Night! Holy Night!" and by Franz Gruber, composer of the tune, "Stille Nacht". In this hymn "the tender, mystical beauty of the Nativity incidents" has awakened the spirit of reverence and devotion in countless adoring hearts. Concerning the composer of the tune, Franz Gruber, it is said: "His life was always greatly circumscribed, and he died at Hallein, in 1863, only about twelve miles from where he was born." *His life was always greatly circumscribed,* and yet his music has gone around the world bringing light and healing and peace to millions of hearts! The Lord of Glory must have smiled with satisfaction on that Christmas night in 1818 when the tenor voice of Franz Gruber first gave forth the melody to the accompaniment of his guitar in an obscure Austrian village. Little did the village schoolmaster realize the inestimable value of the treasure he laid at the feet of Mary's Child that holy night.

We recall the offering laid at His feet by Martin Luther, the author of "Away In a Manger, No Crib For a Bed." The child of a peasant family himself, it fell to his lot to lay at the feet of "the little Lord Jesus" the tenderest and best loved of all the Christmas hymns. This tender and lovely carol, during all the centuries since, "in the several tongues of many lands, has been the lullaby sung over the heads of countless children. This Christmas hymn has been the message to unnumbered little children, by which they have learned to know and to love 'the little Lord Jesus.' "

2. *The Treasures of Poetry*. We think of the tribute of adoration and praise of one of the purest souls who ever lived, John Milton. When he was twenty-one years of age and still a student at Cambridge, he composed the beautiful ode, "On the Morning of Christ's Nativity." The poem was begun on Christmas Day 1629, and completed soon thereafter. Concerning this ode, Hamilton Mabie has written, "When one opens the volume at this great song, it is like going into a church and hearing the organ played by unseen hands; the silence is flooded by a vast music which lifts the heart into the presence of great mysteries." John Bailey, in his little book, "Milton", says of this ode: "the first Christmas night becomes in Milton's [poem] a vision of all time and all space, with heaven in it, and the stars, and the music of the spheres, and the great timeless scheme of redemption . . ." The first two stanzas of the prologue contain the characteristic Miltonic strains of sublime beauty and majestic power.

I.

*This is the month and this the happy morn,*
*Wherein the Son of Heaven's eternal King,*
*Of wedded maid and virgin mother born,*
*Our great redemption from above did bring;*
*For so the holy sages once did sing,*
  *That he our deadly forfeit should release,*
*And with His Father work us a perpetual peace.*

II.

*That glorious form, that light unsufferable,*
*And that far-beaming blaze of majesty,*
*Wherewith he wont at Heaven's high council-table*

*To sit the midst of Trinal Unity,*
*He laid aside, and, here with us to be,*
*Forsook the courts of everlasting day,*
*And chose with us a darksome house of mortal clay.*

The poet's high aim of paying tribute to the "Infant God" is seen in the third stanza:

### III.

*Say, Heavenly Muse, shall not thy sacred vein*
*Afford a present to the Infant God?*
*Hast thou no verse, no hymn, or solemn strain,*
*To welcome him to this his new abode,*
*Now while the heaven by the Sun's team untrod,*
*Hath took no print of the approaching light,*
*And all the spangled host keep watch in squadrons bright?*

With each passing year, the "Golden Treasury" of Christmas poetry becomes larger, richer and more impressive. Hundreds of poems, grand and lowly, rich in sentiment, adoration and devotion are continually pouring forth from worshipful hearts in praise of Him for Whom Christmas is named. From this growing anthology of poetical tributes we select one of the more humble offerings that suggests the kind of gifts Christ wants from His lowly servants. This poem is called "A Christmas Prayer" and was written by the author of many beautiful Christmas poems, Grace Noll Crowell.

*Lord God, I have no great expensive gift*
*To offer to one single soul today,*
*But Lord, dear Lord, if Thou wilt help me lift*
*The burden from some pilgrim on the way,*
*And set his heart rejoicing, I shall be*
*Glad to serve in memory of Thee.*

*I have no glittering jewels I can give,*
*No gleaming satins, but perhaps I may*
*Speak out Thy shining word by which men live,*
*To help some traveler faring on his way;*
*Perhaps I can show kindness to some one*
*Who may have felt that hope and joy were done.*

*These be my gifts. Oh, magnify them Lord,*
*Until they shine like diamonds in the light:*
*The clear illumination of Thy Word,*
*The kindness like a lamp within the night;*
*The eager hand that reaches out and lifts,*
*Accept them Lord, they are my only gifts.*

3. *The Treasures of Story*. Many beautiful Christmas stories have been written. But we can consider only one—the one that stands first among all the Christmas stories outside of the New Testament for its surpassing beauty and abiding truth. On December 7th, 1926, it was my privilege to spend an hour with Henry van Dyke in the study of his home, Avalon, at Princeton, New Jersey. During the course of our conversation, I asked him a question that led him to talk about his story of "The Other Wise Man." I inferred from what he said that he regarded this story as the best thing he had written. "It has been very popular," he said; "more than a million copies have been sold, and it has been published in all of the more important languages of the world. It is a good little story." I did not ask him how he came to write it, for this I knew already from another source. He wrote the story in the year 1896 when he was minister of the Brick Presbyterian Church in New York City. It was his custom each year to write a Christmas story to read to his congregation in place of a sermon. So this story of "The Other Wise Man" was first read to his congregation as a Christmas story and as a substitute for a sermon. It would be well if we could have more such substitutes for sermons! We believe that the story of "The Other Wise Man" has the place of pre-eminence among all the Christmas stories that have been written. And it is a matter deserving of our attention that this great Christian minister, writer, statesman and educator regarded this story as *the best thing he had written*. Henry van Dyke is another rare soul who has laid the best treasures of his mind and heart at the feet of his King.

4. *The Treasures of Art*. What priceless treasures the great artists of the world have laid at His feet! His birth, boyhood, ministry, and passion have been portrayed in the masterpieces of art. The spirit of adoration and loving devotion of those who have labored to give the world these priceless treasures of art is illustrated in the words of Ernst T. Hoffman, the noted German painter. Said he, "When I read again the story of His life and contemplate His teachings, it is as though I were lifted from the valley to the broad table-land, and from thence to successive mountain heights, until

I stand at last upon the highest peak above the clouds, where all is clear and radiant with sunlight, and it has been during these mountain-top experiences that I have seemed to behold His face and have attempted to paint His likeness."

The richest treasures of all center about His Nativity and His Passion. The *Christmas treasures* of art, properly speaking, embrace all of the great masterpieces that have to do with His Nativity. The Annunciation, the Angelic Proclamation to the Shepherds, the Mother and Child, the Holy Family, the Adoration of the Shepherds, the Worship of the Wisemen, the Presentation in the Temple, the Flight into Egypt, all are treated. The wealth of beauty, sentiment, reverence, aspiration, worship, love and sacrifice these treasures of art have given to the world cannot be calculated. But He Who is the Lord of Art must be highly pleased with the humble offerings of His servants.

We are informed there are more than fifty Madonnas that are considered worthy of special mention by the greatest art critics. Among the painters of Madonnas, Raphael stands supreme. Among his greatest are the "Madonna Della Sedia," "Madonna Degli Ansidei," "Madonna Della Candelabra," in London; "Madonna of the Canopy," in the Pitti Palace, Florence; "Madonna Belle Jardiniere (Pretty Gardener), in the Louvre; and the "Sistine Madonna," now in the Dresden Gallery. The "Sistine Madonna" is considered one of the twelve great paintings of the world. It conveys the artist's idea of the Virgin as the Queen of Heaven. She is descending from the clouds and holds the child Jesus in her arms. On either side St. Barbara and St. Sixtus kneel in adoration, and below are two cherubs famous for their beauty. My wife, who saw this painting in Dresden during the summer of 1927, has written for me the following impressions. "As we visited many art galleries throughout Europe and saw one after another of the famous paintings of the Madonna and Child, none of these seemed to satisfy. Some were too fantastically saintly and unreal. Others were too human, too mortal, too realistic. When I expressed this feeling to our conductor, he said, 'Wait till you see the *Sistine Madonna*. I am sure she is the one you are looking for.' Later, in Dresden, Germany, in a room set apart for this one great masterpiece, he stood beside me and whispered, 'There! is she not all you want in a Madonna? She has a faint sadness in her face because she is looking down upon a world of sin and sorrow. But she is smiling, too, because she knows that everything is going to be all right. Here in her arms she holds the Saviour of that world. She is altogether human; altogether divine'."

5. *The Treasures of Music*. The greatest treasure of music to be laid at the feet of the Christ Child is found in Handel's oratorio, *The Messiah*. Handel wrote this oratorio when he was fifty-seven years old, completing it in twenty-four days. It was first produced in Dublin, Ireland, in 1742. *The Messiah* is Handel's greatest work, and ranks first among the great oratorios of the world. Ranking next to it are Mendelssohn's *Elijah* and Haydn's *Creation*. *The Messiah*, we are told, "represents the ripened product of Handel's genius, and reflects the noblest aspirations and most exalted devotion of mankind. Among all his oratorios it retains its original freshness, vigor, and beauty in the highest degree, in that it appeals to the loftiest sentiment and to universal religious devotion."

*The Messiah* is divided into three parts. The first part, with which we are chiefly concerned here, illustrates the longing of the world for the Messiah, prophesies His coming, and announces His birth. Using the text of Scripture throughout, this part contains a beautiful opening recitative by the tenor soloist, *Comfort ye, my people*, and an ornate aria, *Every valley shall be exalted*. The bass recitative, *Thus saith the Lord*, announces the prophecy, and the aria, *But who may abide?*, expresses the human apprehension of the Day of His coming. The aria leads to an exquisite fugal chorus, *And He shall purify*, which is followed by a beautiful contralto aria, *O thou that tellest good tidings to Zion*. One of the finest choruses of the oratorio, *For unto us a Child is born*, precedes a lovely *Pastoral Symphony* by the orchestra, which tells the message of the angels to the shepherds on the plains of Bethlehem, one of the most perfect musical expressions of the spirit of Christmas Eve. The contralto solo, *He shall feed His flock,* is one of the great melodies of all time. There is deathless beauty also in the soprano aria, *Come unto Him, all ye that labor.* The first part closes with another fugal chorus, *His yoke is easy.*

The second part contains the famous *Hallelujah Chorus,* which is the supreme triumph and climax of the oratorio. Concerning this chorus Handel said, "I did think I did see all heaven before me, and the great God Himself." It is interesting to know that eight days before his death, Handel, then totally blind, directed his famous oratorio, *The Messiah,* at Covent Garden, London. This was his last public appearance. It is inspiring and satisfying to think that this great musical genius gave the richest treasure of his soul as an offering to his Saviour, the King of Kings and Lord of Lords.

These are some of the treasures the great spirits of the past have offered to the Christ. What about ourselves? What do we have to bring to Him? Some make the sad mistake of thinking they have nothing to bring. But all of us can give Him our love, our devotion, our talents, our service, our lives, our all. He alone is worthy to receive the best that we are and have. Let us be as wise as the good and great of the past who have given their very best to our common Saviour and King. Let us be the kingly spirits of our day and consecrate our lives and possessions to Christ and His eternal Kingdom.

> *"As they offered gifts most rare*
> *At that manger rude and bare;*
> *So may we with holy joy,*
> *Pure, and free from sin's alloy,*
> *All our costliest treasures bring,*
> *Christ, to Thee, our heavenly King."*

*How They Found the Christ Child*

# BLESSED NIGHT, WHEN FIRST THAT PLAIN

*Blessed night, when first that plain*
*Echoed with the joyful strain,*
*"Peace has come to earth again."*
    *Alleluia!*

*Blessed hills, that heard the song*
*Of the glorious angel throng*
*Swelling all your slopes along.*
    *Alleluia!*

*Happy shepherds, on whose ear*
*Fell the tidings glad and clear,*
*"God to man is drawing near."*
    *Alleluia!*

*Thus revealed to shepherds' eyes,*
*Hidden from the great and wise,*
*Entering earth in lowly guise:*
    *Alleluia!*

*We adore Thee as our King,*
*And to Thee our song we sing;*
*Our best offering to Thee bring.*
    *Alleluia!*

*Blessed Babe of Bethlehem,*
*Owner of earth's diadem,*
*Claim and wear the radiant gem.*
    *Alleluia!*

—REV. HORATIUS BONAR, 1857.

## XII

## HOW THEY FOUND THE CHRIST CHILD

LUKE 2:16, *And they came with haste, and found both Mary and Joseph, and the babe lying in the manger.*

THE more we meditate upon the Christmas Story the more wonderful and meaningful it becomes to us. Its brief pages become filled with living characters; its swiftly changing scenes reveal an orderly and mysterious unity; its natural and commonplace events, as well as its supernatural signs and ineffable intimations, at once give a clear revelation of the simplicity and profundity of the Gospel of Christ. Every dramatic episode is a parable of spiritual truth; every word spoken, whether by heavenly messengers or by plain men and women, is vibrant with meaning; every sign and symbol is a Jacob's Ladder connecting the darkened earth with the eternal glory of heaven. In a wonderful and unique sense, the words of the Christmas Gospel are spirit and life to those who are prepared to receive them.

One singularly inviting and rewarding approach to the truth of Christmas is that of considering the various ways in which the groups we know so well came to find the Christ Child. We immediately discover distinguishing characteristics about these groups of people, as well as marked differences in the ways in which they found the Infant Light. To say that this is accidental or even incidental is to overlook much that is full of meaning and profit. We believe that the Supreme Artist has made every stroke count in the Masterpiece of Christmas. Accordingly, we look for and discover beauty and meaning in every detail of the Picture. We perceive that God has revealed His truths to men in a variety of ways and for different purposes. He has clearly marked the roads that men may take to lead them to Bethlehem and to Mary's Child, the Son of God. Each soul may take the road of his own choosing; the road that best suits his condition and needs. Each may follow the road that appeals to him most. But each must follow the road all the way until he arrives and finds and rejoices and is satisfied.

### I. A Glorious Revelation.

We are quite familiar with the way in which the shepherds found the Infant Saviour—or are we? Perhaps it is better to say that we are familiar with the external features of the story. For there is something of mystery and much that demands rare spiritual insight even about these simple shepherd folk.

The shepherds went to their fields and flocks that night as on many previous nights. They did not expect anything unusual to happen to affect them beyond the ordinary demands and duties of their work. It may be that the stars shone brighter than night; that the clear air was vibrant with suppressed Voices; that the winds stirred the branches softly like the rustle of angels' wings. It may be that the shepherds were strangely sensitive to feelings of keen expectancy and that they communicated these feelings to their flocks until they became unquiet and restless. But certainly the shepherds were totally unprepared for what was to happen before their night vigil ended.

God was watching the shepherds that night even as they were watching their sheep. The hour had come for the curtain to be lifted. God said to the herald angel, "Go on, and deliver My message." Just then the angel appeared to the shepherds, and the glory of the Lord shone round about them. The angel delivered the message from on High and withdrew. A great multitude of the heavenly host sang from the portals of heaven their majestic hymn of glory and peace. The curtain was let down again.

This glorious revelation was granted to the shepherds without any effort on their part. They stayed where they were; they were engaged in their ordinary task; they were exactly where they had been on many nights before this. They were in their own native fields and familiar surroundings when the glory of the Lord broke upon them. The angels sought out the shepherds; the shepherds were not searching for angels but shepherding sheep.

The revelation granted to the shepherds was clear, definite, complete. The messenger told them *Who* was born: "A Saviour, Christ the Lord." He told them *where* to find Him: "in the city of David." He told them *when* to find Him: "this day." He told them *how* to know Him: "Ye shall find a babe wrapped in swaddling clothes, and lying in a manger." He told them *why* the Saviour was born: that "good tidings of great joy" might come "to all the people." The song of the Heavenly Choir revealed to them the ultimate purpose back of it all, namely, that "Glory to God in the highest" might result and that "peace among men" on earth might prevail. What more did the shepherds need to know? They had received all they needed to know until they acted upon the knowledge already given. God's revelations, instructions and directions are always clear enough and definite enough for faith, obedience and action. If we accept and act upon the knowledge we have, God will lead us forward along the path where we may walk in the light even as He is in the light.

All of God's revelations of grace and truth are merciful and gracious, but sometimes they come as a great flood of glory, as a message of surpassing joy, as a song of angel voices when the night is darkest and when human expectation and hope are at lowest ebb. We recall the experience of Peter. In the Book of Acts we read that Herod Agrippa, grandson of Herod the Great, had put forth his bloody hands to afflict certain of the church. He had killed James the brother of John with the sword. He had seized Peter and put him in prison. At midnight Peter was sleeping between two soldiers, bound with two chains. And behold, an angel of the Lord stood by him, and a light shone in the cell. The chains fell off, the gates opened, and Peter was free! We do not forget that a praying church was the human factor in the miraculous deliverance of Peter. Even so God can and does visit, redeem, and deliver His people whensoever and wheresoever He chooses to demonstrate His power and reveal His glory.

## II. *A Spiritual Preparation.*

God did reveal the good tidings of great joy to the shepherds by surprising them with His grace and glory, but all this would have availed nothing had not the shepherds acted upon the revelation granted to them. That they were especially worthy to receive the revelation is clearly seen in their subsequent conduct. The record is equally definite and complete as to the response the shepherds made to this heavenly truth. They *accepted* the message as a *divine* revelation: "which the Lord hath made known to us." They *believed* the message to be *true*: "Let us go . . . and see this thing that is come to pass." They were *obedient* to the heavenly vision: "Let us now go even unto Bethlehem." They were *rewarded* for their faith and obedience: "And they came with haste, and found . . . the babe lying in the manger." They *shared* the good tidings of the Saviour's birth with others: "they made known" and "the shepherds returned, glorifying and praising God."

Thus while we give glory to God for His gracious revelation to the shepherds, yet at the same time we must not fail to note the special fitness of the shepherds in being thus chosen and honored. These humble men were evidently prepared in heart and spirit to be faithful recipients and witnesses of the tidings of the Saviour's birth. James Stalker, in "The Life of Christ," tells why the angels came to the shepherds with their heavenly message. "And seeking the most worthy hearts to which they might communicate it, they found them in these simple shepherds, living the life of contemplation and prayer in the suggestive fields where Jacob had kept his flocks, where Boaz and Ruth had been wedded, and David, the great Old Testament type, had spent his youth, and there by the study of the secrets and needs of their own hearts, learning far more of the nature of the Saviour who was to come than the Pharisee amidst the religious pomp of the temple, or the scribe burrowing without the seeing eye among the prophecies of the Old Testament."

We might ask the question why the scribes and Pharisees who were the religious leaders of the nation did not receive the tidings of Messiah's birth in place of the shepherds. We might inquire why Herod, the king of Judaea, did not see the Star of Bethlehem instead of the Wise-men from the Gentile world. We might wonder why some high priest like Annas or Caiaphas did not have the privilege of holding the little babe who was the Glory of Israel in his arms instead of the lowly and devout Simeon. To raise these and similar questions is to answer them. The scribes and Pharisees, King Herod, the high priests and others of like character were totally unprepared, morally and spiritually, to receive the announcements, tidings and blessings of the Saviour's coming. God could not use them; He did not use them in welcoming and receiving His Gift of Love to the world.

Hugh Thompson Kerr in "Old Things New" retells an incident from Bernard Shaw's "Saint Joan" that is most significant. Following the coronation of King Charles of France in the cathedral, Joan tells the king and the Archbishop that the heavenly voices are bidding her lead the armies of France on to victory and she is sure that if only the king will not falter, success will come. But the king, impatient and incredulous and worldly, replied, "O, your voices; your voices. Why don't the voices come to me. I am the king, not you." And Joan answered, "They do come to you, but you do not hear them. You have not sat in the field in the evening and listened for them. When the Angelus rings you cross yourself and have done with it; but if you prayed from your heart and listened to the thrilling of the bells in the air after they had stopped ringing you would hear voices as well as I do."

The shepherds represent the humble class of people in all lands and ages who endeavor to walk humbly with their God and seek His glory in the commonplace and do His will in the everyday tasks and duties and relationships of life. They belong to the class of hearers Jesus described in the Parable of the Sower: "these are such as in an honest and good heart, having heard the word, hold it fast, and bring forth fruit with patience." The great majority of Jesus' disciples then and in all the generations since have been made up of simple-hearted men and women of faith and goodness like the shepherds.

## III. *A Faithful Declaration.*

The shepherds of Bethlehem were the first to receive the angelic tidings of the Saviour's birth. And yet another distinction belongs to them. They were also the first witnesses of the Christmas Gospel; the first to tell others the good tidings of great joy they had received. They lost no time in doing this. Of course the first to hear the testimony of the shepherds were Mary and Joseph. What a holy place the stable of Bethlehem becomes! What a strange pulpit! What Spirit-filled messengers! What eager listeners! Was there ever a more beautiful Christmas service than this? No, there could not be; for this was Christmas itself. The earnest shepherds related in low and awe-inspiring tones the message they had heard from the angels. Mary and Joseph drank in every word. They knew these things of course from the previous revelations granted to them by the angels of God. But their hearts were lifted up in joy and wonderment that their hopes had been confirmed by this latest revelation of heavenly tidings to the shepherds.

Faithfully, honestly, truthfully the shepherds told the story even as it had been given unto them. Their message was simple and complete. They were true witnesses; the only kind God can use as His spokesmen. They knew that the Lord had given them their message, and they were moved by divine inspiration to declare it to others. Their's was the heaven-born integrity and compulsion that marked the witnessing of Peter and John when they declared: "we cannot but speak the things which we saw and heard." All faithful witnesses to the truth as it is in Jesus need these qualities so conspicuously present in the hearts of the lowly shepherds.

The message of the shepherds produced wonderment in the hearts of all who heard. There were evidently a number of folk in and around Bethlehem who heard what the shepherds had to tell. For the record reads, *"And all that heard it wondered."* Mary and Joseph were not the only ones to hear their word. There were other pious people whose names we do not know. There were other humble hearts ready to receive the Christ Child. This same encouraging truth is quietly revealed in the record of the presentation of the Child Jesus in the temple. Concerning good old Anna it is said, "And coming up at that very hour she gave thanks unto God, and spoke of him *to all them that were looking for the redemption of Jerusalem."* Simeon and Anna were not the only saints in the city of Jerusalem. They are the only ones whose names we know, but there was the larger company of quiet and devout people who were waiting and watching for the coming of their King. All witnesses of the Evangel should be guided and encouraged by the vision granted by the Lord to Paul at Corinth: "Be not afraid, but speak and hold not thy peace: for I am with thee, and no man shall set on thee to harm thee: *for I have much people in this city"* (Acts 18:9-10).

We do well to remember how the testimony of the shepherds was treasured in the heart of the mother. We are told that Mary kept all these sayings of the shepherds, "pondering them in her heart." With her profound sense of spiritual insight and her great capacity for feeling, Mary's soul would again be lifted up in joy and exultation as her spirit rejoiced in God her Saviour. It is said of the ancient Greek painters that when they wished to portray a scene that evoked indescribable emotion, they would put a veil over the face of the one so deeply moved. So the evangelist Luke, under the impulse of a higher inspiration, draws a veil over the scene of the mother's emotion, and permits the reader to imagine the feeling of unspeakable joy that filled the heart of Mary. "But Mary kept all these sayings, pondering them in her heart."

Thus the understanding heart of Mary became the next depository of the sweetest story ever told. The angels of God proclaimed the message to the shepherds; the faithful shepherds repeated it to the mother; the mother preserved it for the evangelist, and the evangelist gave it to the world. The world has taken this story to its heart, and continues to publish abroad its meaning and message in a multitude of ways. Music, art, poetry, drama, religion, all have been brought under the influence of its spell and have contributed their resources towards making the message more real and regnant in human life. The chief mission of every believer and receiver of the Christmas Gospel is to become a faithful and true witness to its message of love and light and life.

The shepherds, we know, declared their faith and manifested their joy in their every day life. They "returned, glorifying and praising God"; they returned to their homes and sheepfolds, to their every day tasks and relationships with the spirit of love and service dominant in their lives. The shepherds found the true meaning of Christmas not only in receiving the glorious revelation of the angels, but also in sharing the good news with their fellowmen. The revelation was granted that their faithful witnessing might follow. Christmas has two sides: the side of divine inspiration and the side of human response. Our Christmas experience can be full and complete only as we follow the shepherds in joyously receiving the heavenly tidings and in faithfully proclaiming these tidings to others.

> "I love to tell the story;
>   'Tis pleasant to repeat
> What seems, each time I tell it,
>   More wonderfully sweet.
> I love to tell the story,
>   For some have never heard
> The message of salvation
>   From God's own holy word."

*The Pondering Heart*

## AWAY IN A MANGER

*Away in a manger, no crib for a bed,*
*The little Lord Jesus laid down His sweet head;*
*The stars in the bright sky looked down where He lay,*
*The little Lord Jesus asleep on the hay.*

*The cattle are lowing, the Baby awakes,*
*But little Lord Jesus, no crying He makes.*
*I love Thee, Lord Jesus, look down from the sky,*
*And stay by my cradle till morning is nigh.*

*Be near me, Lord Jesus; I ask Thee to stay*
*Close by me forever, and love me, I pray.*
*Bless all the dear children in Thy tender care,*
*And fit us for heaven to live with Thee there.*

—MARTIN LUTHER, 1530.

## XIII

## THE PONDERING HEART

LUKE 2:19, *But Mary kept all these sayings, pondering them in her heart.*

IN THE providence of God there was one person who knew the meaning of Christmas better than any other. That person was the virgin Mary, mother of the Saviour Child. Hence, it goes without saying that if we are to understand the real mystery of Christmas we must come to see and feel its meaning through the eyes and heart of the Saviour's mother.

At the time of Jesus' birth the little town of Bethlehem was crowded with visitors and filled with confusion and excitement. It was like a great home-coming occasion for those who belonged to the house and family of David. The matter of their lodging being cared for, the visitors could give themselves over without restraint to the pleasures and opportunities the occasion provided. They could meet and mingle with old friends and acquaintances; spend the time of their brief sojourn in discussing the news of the day and recalling memories of past good times together. It was a glad, gay, busy, and care-free occasion such as most holidays afford.

Only a few immediate relatives and close friends paid any attention to the distress of Mary and Joseph. When Mary's child was born the news quickly spread throughout the village. The women all knew it first and told their husbands. But the busy crowds of visitors gave it little thought. "Did you hear that a poor peasant woman from Nazareth gave birth to a son last night?" "Yes, and what a pity she had to go through such an ordeal at this time, and in such a place!"

"Why, they say that she had to dress the baby with her own hands, and lay him in a manger!" An interesting item of news a bit unusual, to be sure, but for most of the visitors just a means of passing the time of day. When they went back to their homes after completing the business of the enrolment they remained in complete ignorance of the meaning of the event that had come to pass in Bethlehem while they were there. Although it was the greatest event of all time, yet those who were closest to it knew nothing of its meaning!

However, there were a few who gained impressions which remained with them all their lives. Some shepherds came in from the nearby fields, where they had been keeping their flocks by night, with a wonderful story to tell. They found Mary and Joseph, and the babe lying in the manger, and related what the angel had said to them concerning this child. "And the shepherds returned, glorifying and praising God for all the things that they had heard and seen, even as it was spoken unto them." Of course they never forgot the experience of that wonderful night when the angels of heaven spoke good tidings to them and sang their hymn of glory and of peace.

The shepherds repeated again and again the saying of the angel. The people who heard their story were filled with wonder and astonishment. "But Mary kept all these sayings, pondering them in her heart." She was neither surprised nor astonished as were the inhabitants of Bethlehem. She and her husband Joseph had both been prepared for these miraculous events by the revelation of the angels. Mary did not publish abroad her impressions at this time, but kept them quietly in her heart.

## I. The Spiritual Insight of the Pondering Heart.

Mary was much given to meditation. She was a quiet, thoughtful woman with a deep spiritual nature. She possessed that reticence and poise, that innate quietude of spirit which is the real charm of woman. Her habitual manner was characterized by the kind of silence that is golden. Her meditative nature was given the fullest opportunity to express itself during those eventful days! Mary had a lot to think about!

Her young life suddenly became filled with a kaleidoscopic series of events sufficient to test the equanimity of the most heroic in spirit. The quiet intrusion of the Annunciation Angel upon her peaceful life in Nazareth; the memorable visit with her kinswoman Elisabeth for three months; the return to Nazareth; the trying days and nights for six months under strained relations with Joseph; the decree concerning the census, and the long and difficult journey to the City of David; the inhospitable reception at Bethlehem; the birth of her first-born in the stable; the coming of the shepherds; the journey to the Temple six weeks later, and the strange words of Simeon; the sojourn in Bethlehem until the coming of the Wise Men; the hasty flight into Egypt; the sad news of the slaughter of the babies of Bethlehem; the return to the land of Israel and warning against staying there; the eventful return to Nazareth. What a strange course of events for a humble peasant maiden who had lived a quiet and sheltered life in Galilee!

And Mary kept all these things, pondering them in her heart. She revolved them over and over again in her mind seeking to comprehend the mystery of God's dealings with her and striving to understand the larger meaning for humanity. She pondered deeply over the revelations of the angels and the things that God had showed her through the words of His servants. Her main purpose was to get a true picture of the Christ in her mind and heart and a clear understanding of His mission in the world. Her song, the "Magnificat," admirably reflects how well she understood the mercy of God and the saving, transforming mission of His Son.

This will be the aim of all who seek to know the meaning of Christmas. The aim and intent of all pondering hearts will be to recapture the feelings and experiences that were born in the hearts of those who shared the first Christmas. Their purpose will be to get a truer portrait of the Son of God in their minds, and a deeper love for Him in their hearts.

Mary's way of the pondering heart is one of the indispensable ways of discovering the true Christmas. It is the way our busy, bustling world most commonly disregards and abuses. This is a restless age, an age of unceasing activity, an age little disposed to spiritual meditation. It is a voluble age, filled with voluble people, noises, sounds, broadcasts. Some one is always broadcasting! A world of talkative, expressive people, most of whom have very little to express! The deepest feelings of the human heart lead to silence; the most lasting impressions do not explode and disappear in a cloud of volubility!

To many people Christmas is merely a busy holiday season, crammed with activities, social events, and a dizzy round of pleasures. When it is all over they find themselves left with a big headache and a curious let-down feeling. They heave a sigh of relief and are somewhat sensitive to a feeling of gratitude that, after all, Christmas comes but once a year. How many repeat the experience of Mary and secure a firmer hold upon the spiritual values of Christmas cannot be known; for they, like Mary, are not inclined to become voluble concerning the deep things they have felt within their souls.

## II. *The Treasures of the Pondering Heart.*

We can be assured that the Christmas treasures we will keep will belong to the realm of the heart and of the spirit. In Mary's experience the angels went away again into heaven; the shepherds withdrew and went back to their sheepfolds; the Wise Men presented their costly gifts and departed; Simeon and Anna soon passed from the earthly Temple to the heavenly Jerusalem; the swiftly moving scenes of new lands and peoples passed before her eyes, but the wonderful revelations concerning the Saviour Child were treasured in her mother heart for ever. It is a very strange thing that, so far as we know, Jesus never returned to Bethlehem, the scene of His birth. But we may be sure that Mary the mother made many a pilgrimage in memory to the place where she laid her firstborn Son in the lowly manger.

The way of the pondering heart is our road to Bethlehem. We may go there in our thoughts as we meditate upon the story of Christmas. Like the shepherds of old, we must *resolve* to make this pilgrimage. It requires an act of will and determination on our part: *"Let us* now go even unto Bethlehem." Many will not go; they will be too busy with the outward paraphernalia of Christmas. But *we* must determine to go; we must go *now,* before it is too late. It is not an *easy* matter to go; we must take time; we must make sacrifices; we must put aside pressing matters. But we must go, *even* though the way be difficult, if we are to find the Christ and the new life He has for us.

The true perception and heart-felt understanding of the Christmas message is worth infinitely more than all the glitter and splendor this passing world has to offer. Do not forget that Mary and Joseph lived in a thriving, busy, colorful world. Henry van Dyke, in his story "Even Unto Bethlehem", describes the world pageantry the eyes of this rustic couple frequently rested upon from their quiet retreat in Nazareth. "Roman soldiers in glittering ranks, armored and helmeted, with bright eagle-standards shining above their serried spears. Proud horsemen on their Arab stallions. Rich merchants and noblemen in their cushioned litters. Rumbling chariots of brass and gilded wood. Gaily-decorated mules, their collars studded with turquoises and their pack-saddles heaped with crates and boxes. Pattering asses moving under their huge loads like patient curious insects. Scornful, ungainly camels swaying silently along on their padded feet, fastened one to another by ropes or jingling chains, like lines of barges in a tow, laden with corn from the Hauran, silks and swords from Damascus, spices and fragrant woods from Arabia, sweet fruits from the orchards and gardens of Galilee, ornaments and jewels and carven-work from the Greek cities of the Dekapolis. All the wealth and splendor of earth poured along that paved road with its three tracks, each twelve feet wide, divided by upright stones."

But Mary and Joseph belonged to the "plain, hard-working, high-thoughted folk" of Galilee. "They were content in poverty, since they were enriched in soul by the promises made of old to the people of Israel. They were happy in obscurity and not cast down, since they knew that they were of the house and lineage of David from whose royal seed the Messiah was to come. They could let the pomp and vanity of the world stream by below them without an envious thought." Those who know the secret of the pondering heart are spiritual descendants of Mary and Joseph. They look upon the glittering world of commerce, traffic, and material splendor "without an envious thought" because they know they possess the true and lasting treasures of God's mercy and salvation. They can echo the affirmation of Tennyson: "I know because I have felt." The pondering heart is not to be deceived!

## III. *The Fruits of the Pondering Heart.*

In due time, Mary gave to the world the ripened fruits of her pondering heart. And what an incomparably rich and precious contribution she has made to the spiritual wealth of humanity! For it was through the heart of Mary that God gave to the world the most beautiful story it possesses — the Infancy Gospel of the opening chapters of Luke. None other than she could have revealed the intimate and personal happenings that are recorded in connection with the Saviour's birth. Humanly speaking, we would know nothing about the Annunciation, the angels and the shepherds, the manger birth, the visit to the Temple, and Jesus' childhood in Nazareth had not these precious stories been given to us by the mother who had long treasured them in her heart.

Take out of the world and away from the spirit of humanity all of the Christmas music and meaning that can be traced to Mary's Gospel of the Infant Saviour, and our lives would be immeasurably impoverished and benighted. What would Christmas be if we could not kneel in worship at the manger-cradle? if the skies were not vocal with angel music? if there were no humble shepherds praising and glorifying God for the wonderful things they had heard and seen?

if there were no beautiful young mother holding her precious baby to her heart? if we did not know that God so loved us that He gave His only begotten Son to save us and to give us eternal life? The heritage we have received from the pondering heart of the mother of our Lord is infinitely more valuable than all the material gifts of this world piled together. "For what is a man profited, if he shall gain the whole world, and lose his own soul? or what shall a man give in exchange for his soul?" The soul of Christmas *comes from* and *resides in* the pondering heart. We must be careful to guard our spiritual heritage from the destructive moths of commercialism, the corrosive rust of materialism, the impoverishing thieves of agnosticism. "For where thy treasure is, there will thy heart be also." The treasure of the heart is to be found in the resources of wisdom, grace, and love in Jesus Christ, our Lord.

The most valuable contribution any one of us can make to the world will be found to partake of the nature of Mary's bequest. Our greatest contribution will be spiritual and not material. The finest gold we are permitted to put in the grain-sacks of human lives is the gold of spirituality. Peter said to the lame man outside of the beautiful gate of the Temple, "Silver and gold have I none; but what I have, that give I thee. In the name of Jesus Christ of Nazareth, walk." And we all understand that Peter gave to his brother man the greatest possible gift.

It is comparatively easy to bestow attractive and acceptable material gifts providing you have three things: the spirit of good will, money, and good taste. But it is not easy to impart spiritual gifts to people who sorely need them but do not want them; to people who, like the lame beggar, are asking for a paltry sum of money when they need the ability to rise up and walk; to people who are blinded by the glare and glitter of material things so that they do not perceive the true worth and reward of spiritual values.

Our world stands in greatest need of spiritual ideals, convictions, and realities. The greatest benefactor is he who can best supply our human need. In this sense, Jesus Christ is the Saviour of the world. He is the Saviour from sin, the Bread of Life, the Light of the World, the Shepherd of the Sheep. Consequently, His true disciples, His loyal followers are those best fitted to supply the world with what it needs most. Before they can do this, they must know Christ and live in fellowship with Him; they must meditate upon His teachings until these become a vital part of character and conduct; they must become so filled with His spirit of compassion and love that their lives will overflow in kindness and good deeds to others. "A new commandment I give unto you, that ye love one another; even as I have loved you, that ye also love one another. By this shall all men know that ye are my disciples, if ye have love one to another." Even so will our meditation upon the meaning of Christmas find a larger and sweeter fruitage in human life, to the praise of the glory of His grace.

*Kings and Shepherds*

## ONCE IN ROYAL DAVID'S CITY

*Once in royal David's city*
  *Stood a lowly cattle-shed*
*Where a mother laid her Baby*
  *In a manger for His bed:*
*Mary was that mother mild,*
*Jesus Christ her little Child.*

*He came down to earth from heaven*
  *Who is God and Lord of all,*
*And His shelter was a stable,*
  *And His cradle was a stall:*
*With the poor, and mean, and lowly,*
*Lived on earth our Saviour Holy.*

*And, through all His wondrous childhood*
  *He would honor and obey,*
*Love and watch the lowly maiden*
  *In whose gentle arms He lay:*
*Christian children all must be*
*Mild, obedient, good as He.*

*For He is our childhood's Pattern,*
  *Day by day like us He grew,*
*He was little, weak and helpless,*
  *Tears and smiles like us He knew:*
*And He feeleth for our sadness,*
*And He shareth in our gladness.*

*And our eyes at last shall see Him,*
  *Through His own redeeming love;*
*For that Child so dear and gentle*
  *Is our Lord in heaven above,*
*And He leads His children on,*
*To the place where He is gone.*

*Not in that poor lowly stable,*
  *With the oxen standing by,*
*We shall see Him, but in heaven,*
  *Set at God's right hand on high;*
*When like stars His children crowned*
*All in white shall wait around.*
              —Mrs. Cecil F. Alexander, 1848.

## XIV

*12/27/53*

### KINGS AND SHEPHERDS

MATTHEW 2:1, *Now when Jesus was born in Bethlehem of Judaea in the days of Herod the king,
behold, Wise-men from the east came to Jerusalem . . .*

LUKE 2:8, *And there were shepherds in the same
country abiding in the field, and keeping watch
by night over their flock.*

THE Evangelists, Matthew and Luke, have given to the
world two matchless pictures of the events attending the
birth of the Saviour Child. Matthew has depicted the regal
and magnificent scene of the visit of the Wise Men of the
east. Luke has portrayed the humble and beautiful scene of
the coming of the shepherds. These unpretentious yet inimi-
table portrayals drawn by the Evangelists have inspired the
poets, artists, and musicians of the world to use their art in
trying to enlarge and enrich and make more real these wonderful scenes. As a result, we have many masterpieces of
poetry, painting and music conceived by the great artists of
Christendom. The great poets such as Milton, Shakespeare,
Tennyson, Browning, Longfellow, Lowell, Markham, Henry
van Dyke, and many others have written beautiful poems on
the theme of the Nativity. The great painters such as Cor-
regio, Bellini, Veronese, Memling, Titian, Raphael, and others have lavished their skill in depicting scenes of the Madonna and Child, the Adoration of the Magi, and the Visit of
the Shepherds. Our hymn writers and composers have given

us the words and music that keep the whole world singing the Christmas carols that shall never die.

The two pictures drawn by Matthew and Luke are very different in character. We study them not by way of comparison but by way of contrast. This study of contrasts reveals a wealth of meaning as to the significance of the two pictures. Let us look on the one picture and then on the other with the aim of perceiving new beauty and truth in the original portraits of Christmas.

## I. *The Kings of the East.*

A halo of mystery surrounds the Wise Men from the east and a cloud of glory overshadows them. Like the great priest Melchizedek, they have neither beginning nor ending of days. They appear out of the mysterious east, pass swiftly through the opening scenes of the Gospel drama and are lost at once in the unknown. Matthew does not tell us the number of the Wise Men, nor their names, nor specifically whence they came. Tradition, story, and romance have been busy with this theme and the result is that in the minds of many people there is a mixture of fancy and fact. It is commonly supposed that these Wise Men were kings; that they were three in number, and that they came from Greece, India, and Egypt. In story they have been given the names of Caspar, Melchior, and Balthasar.

But from the Gospel record only the following facts can be ascertained. The term "Wise Men" is a translation of the Greek word "magi" which was applied to Oriental seers, astrologers, priests, and wise-men. They came from the east, a general term which may include Arabia and Persia. The oldest opinion is that they came from Arabia, but the more general belief is that they came from Persia. We infer that they were three in number from the fact that three gifts were offered to the Saviour, namely, gold, frankincense, and myrrh. They came to Jerusalem seeking information concerning Him Who was "born King of the Jews." They had previously seen "his star in the east" and had come to worship Him.

Herod sent the Wise Men to Bethlehem after he had learned from the Jews where the Christ was to be born. The Wise Men, guided by the star which went before them, arrived at Bethlehem, found the child with Mary his mother and presented their costly gifts to Him. Then, being warned of God in a dream not to return to Herod, they departed into their own country another way.

In looking for the elements of this story that have a deep and abiding religious significance we need to think of what it meant for these Wise Men to come and worship the Child Jesus. If tradition is correct in stating that these Wise Men were kings, then we have the very significant fact that as rulers and princes they came to render homage to the King of Kings. These royal travelers represent the rich and the powerful of earth. Their coming to Bethlehem is like a royal procession. They are clothed with kingly robes and their retinue is noble and magnificent. There is nothing that suggests poverty or humble circumstances. The gifts they offer are princely gifts fit for a King.

The whole scene tends to accentuate the kingly and sovereign attributes of Jesus, the Messiah. Matthew's Gospel is the Gospel of the King. Matthew does not give any hint of the lowly babe wrapped in swaddling clothes and lying in a manger with the humble shepherds gathered round. On the contrary, he pictures these wealthy nobles opening their treasures and presenting costly gifts to the One Who was worthy of the homage of the greatest of earth. Matthew proclaims the birth of Jesus in the words of the prophet:

> *"And thou Bethlehem, land of Judah,*
> *Art in no wise least among the princes of Judah:*
> *For out of thee shall come forth a governor,*
> *Who shall be shepherd of my people Israel."*

To Matthew, therefore, the birth of Jesus meant the coming of the Messiah, the King of Kings, and Lord of Lords.

Hence, the abiding significance of the presence of the kings of the east is that Christ is worthy to receive the worship, devotion, praise, love, and treasure of the greatest, the richest, and the most powerful of earth. To Him every knee shall bow, and every tongue confess that He is Lord of all, to the glory of God the Father.

Again, we find something of great religious significance in the fact that these Wise Men were representatives of the Gentile world. They did not belong to the Jewish nation; they were Gentiles. And as such, it was thought, at least by the materialistically-minded Jews, that they would not be benefited by the coming of the Messiah. But we know from the teachings of Jesus and from the development of Christianity that the Gospel is for the Gentiles as well as the Jews; that Christ is the Saviour of the whole world. But what is known to us was not known to the people of the east when Christ was born. Hence it is a fact of startling significance that these Gentiles should be concerned about the birth of Christ, and that they should accomplish such a long journey to worship Him and offer Him gifts. Of course the event is prophetic; it is a fore-gleam of the not far distant time when, as a result of the broad comprehension of the Gospel of Christ by the Apostle Paul and others, the Gentiles should be brought into the fellowship of the Christian Church.

Once more, these Wise Men of the east represent the intelligentsia, the intellectual searchers after truth. They were magi, seers, astrologers, Persian priests, perhaps. They were learned in all the science and philosophy of their time. They were searchers after the highest in the religion of the Gentile world. If followers of Zoroaster they worshipped light; they worshipped the stars as "the thoughts of the Eternal." As they stood night after night out under the broad, blue Persian skies and beheld the starry hosts, they communed with the Creator of these myriads of gleaming suns and longed for closer fellowship with Him. They worshipped light and they were seeking for the greater Light, even for Him Who was to be the Light of the World. And because they were seeking they found the object of their search. Their worship of the stars, the highest that they knew, finally brought them to the end of their quest. For there came a time when a special star appeared in their Orient sky and eventually guided them to Bethlehem where the young Child was. And when they found

Him Who was the Bright and Morning Star they rejoiced with exceeding great joy. The story is a solemn lesson of warning to all those who are engaged in scientific researches and philosophical speculations that unless their seeking for truth leads them to Jesus Christ and to worshipful devotion to Him, their quest is vain—their quest is vain. It is also a hopeful message of inspiration and encouragement to those who are sincerely following the light they have to the best of their ability. For if they follow the starlight that guides them through the darkness of night, they shall be led at last to the dawning of the new day wherein the Sun of Righteousness shall shine upon them with saving light.

## II. *The Shepherds of Bethlehem.*

Luke makes no mention of the visit of the Wise Men, but tells the simple and beautiful story of the shepherds. There is nothing of great mystery about the shepherds. The section of the country around Bethlehem was a pastoral country and shepherds with their flocks were familiar scenes of every day life. It would have been a surprising thing *not* to find shepherds around Bethlehem; they belonged to the landscape. Moreover, these shepherds were not foreigners from distant lands. They were Israelites; they belonged to that country, and they dwelt among their own people. They belonged to the humble class of people. They were not kings or rulers, as were the Wise Men; neither were they wealthy nor powerful. They were poor and humble folk belonging, as we say, to the class of common people. There is no record that the shepherds carried gifts to the Saviour Child; they were too poor for that.

The story simply tells us that while the shepherds watched their flocks by night, an angel of the Lord appeared and said to them, "Be not afraid; for behold, I bring you good tidings of great joy which shall be to all the people: for there is born to you this day in the city of David a Saviour, who is Christ the Lord. And this is the sign unto you: Ye shall find a babe wrapped in swaddling clothes, and lying in a manger." Then there appeared with the angel a host of the radiant, shining ones, praising God and saying, "Glory to God in the highest, And on earth peace among men in whom he is well pleased." Straightway the shepherds came to Bethlehem and found Mary and Joseph, and the babe lying in the manger. They related the wonderful things that had befallen them and returned to their flocks, glorifying and praising God for all the things they had heard and seen.

We cannot fail to note the vivid contrast between Matthew's story of the Wise Men and Luke's story of the shepherds. Matthew's picture is of kings arrayed in flowing robes, with royal mien, offering their costly gifts to the Christ Child. Luke's picture is of lowly shepherds, clad in humble homespun garments, with no gifts in their hands, but only wonderment, awe and adoration on their honest countenances. Luke's Gospel is the Gospel of humanity, and this scene impresses upon our minds the fact that the Christmas message is for all people, no matter how poor or humble or needy. Indeed, the angel said to the shepherds, "I bring you good tidings of great joy which shall be *to all the people*." And, as if in answer to the great cry of the needy millions of human beings, the angel announced "for there is born to you this day in the city of David a Saviour, who is Christ the Lord." That is precisely what all poor, humble and distressed people need—a Saviour, One Who is the Good Shepherd of His people.

How fitting it was that the angel's announcement should have been made to shepherds! For he announced the birth of One Who was to be the Good Shepherd of all the lost sheep. And it was especially appropriate that the glad tidings should first be heard in the place where David had kept his father's flocks, and where he learned by heart the gentle words of the Shepherd Psalm. We wonder whether these shepherds who saw the babe in the manger were present thirty years later when Jesus was saying to His people: "I am the door of the sheep; I am the good shepherd; I know my sheep, and mine own know me; I lay down my life for the sheep." This is the message of Christmas; this is the message the angels of heaven desire all humble and needy people to remember, that there was born to them on Christmas day a Saviour Who is Christ the Lord, the Great Shepherd of all the sheep.

It is recorded that the shepherds returned, glorifying and praising God. They returned to their homes and to their sheepfolds to resume their care over their flocks. But they returned as changed men. They went back to their daily tasks with a new joy, a new peace, and a new song in their hearts. They could never forget the song the angels had sung that wonderful night. And so they carried the spirit of Christmas in their hearts. Their return was equally important with their coming. For what would it have profited them if they had come to the manger and gone away without being changed men? And what will Christmas mean to us and to the world if it is only a day on the calendar? Christmas is a spirit, a message, a life that we are to carry with us throughout the year. Following our spiritual feast at Christmas time, it is our privilege and responsibility to return to our humble walks of life, to our occupations and duties, glorifying and praising God for all the blessings we have received in Christ Jesus.

Of course Matthew and Luke exalt the one Saviour and Lord. They suggest in different ways the abundance of truth and grace to be found in Him. He is the Saviour of all men: ruler and subject, classes and masses, rich and poor, learned and unlearned, high and low. He receives all who come to Him, and He gives to all salvation and eternal life. In the beautiful chapel at Princeton University the great western window symbolizes the influence of Christ upon learning. "In the center is the lovely scene of the Nativity, and at the cradle of the Christ Child two processions meet. On the left, coming out of the mystery of light, are the shepherds, the prophets, the kings, and priests of ancient Scripture. On the right, led by the wise men, come the philosophers and theologians, Aquinas, Calvin, Edwards; the poets, Homer, Virgil, Dante, Chaucer, Shakespeare; the scientists, Bacon and Aristotle; the statesmen, Augustus and Justinian, until the whole space is filled; and the legend of the story in glass is,

'I came that they may have life, and may have it more abundantly'."

Let us make the spiritual pilgrimage the shepherds and the Wise Men made. Let us claim and realize the promise God has given: "There is born *to you this day* . . . a Saviour who is Christ the Lord." We can make this journey to the House of Bread by the strange miracle of receiving Christ in our hearts as the Bread of Life. We have tried to suggest this truth in a few verses entitled, "Bethlehem."

*It isn't far to Bethlehem*
  *Where lies the new-born King;*
*It isn't far to Bethlehem*
  *Where holy angels sing.*

*The Wise Men saw the guiding star*
  *That led them where He lay;*
*The shepherds heard the heavenly song*
  *That brought the better day.*

*We, too, may go to Bethlehem*
  *And find the Saviour Child;*
*We, too, may hear the angels sing*
  *Their hymns of mercy mild.*

*Our hearts are God's new Bethlehem*
  *Where Christ is born anew —*
*It isn't far to Bethlehem*
  *If He is born in you!*

*The Light of Christmas*

# THE RACE THAT LONG IN DARKNESS PINED

*The race that long in darkness pined*
*Have seen a glorious Light;*
*The people dwell in day, who dwelt*
*In death's surrounding night.*

*To hail Thy rise, Thou better Sun,*
*The gathering nations come,*
*Joyous as when the reapers bear*
*The harvest-treasures home.*

*For Thou our burden hast removed,*
*And quelled the oppressor's sway,*
*Quick as the slaughtered squadrons fell*
*In Midian's evil day.*

*To us a Child of Hope is born,*
*To us a Son is given;*
*Him shall the tribes of earth obey,*
*Him all the hosts of heaven.*

*His Name shall be the Prince of Peace,*
*For evermore adored,*
*The Wonderful, the Counsellor,*
*The great and mighty Lord.*

*His power increasing still shall spread,*
*His reign no end shall know:*
*Justice shall guard His throne above,*
*And peace abound below.*

—Rev. John Morison, 1781.

## XV

## THE LIGHT OF CHRISTMAS

John 1:4, *In him was life; and the life was the light of men.*

THE Light of Christmas—what a glorious fact it is! What an alluring thought for contemplation! What a cheering experience to dwell in this holy light! Christmas is pre-eminently the Festival of Light. Other holy days in the Christian calendar have their special emblems, but Christmas is distinguished by its array of lights. The world of nature itself is in harmony with the Festival of Light, for the lengthening light of day once more begins to lessen the darkness of night. Myriads of artificial lights of all colors, shapes and sizes appear. Candle-lights softly glow in great cathedrals, stately churches, and lowly chapels. A million Christmas trees are sprinkled with tiny colored lights that shine like jewels. Homes, streets, shops, stores, and all public places of business and amusement are gaily bedecked with strings of lights, clusters of lights, rows of lights, patterns of lights, with all imaginable arrangements of lights. Every passer-by, however poor, lonely or lost he may be, may feast his eyes upon the lights of Christmas and cheer his soul with their friendly glow.

More than all this, Christmas stands for *real* light, for spiritual light, for the light of life. In far-off ages the advent of Messiah was predicted in terms of this life-giving light. Isaiah's prophecies are especially striking. "The people that walked in darkness have seen a great light: they that dwell in the land of the shadow of death, upon them hath the light shined" (Isaiah 9:2). "Arise, shine; for thy light is come, and the glory of Jehovah is risen upon thee" (Isaiah 60:1). "And nations shall come to thy light, and kings to the brightness of thy rising" (Isaiah 60:3). The final strains of prophecy as voiced by Zacharias and Simeon contained the same note. "Whereby the dayspring from on high hath visited us, to give light to them that sit in darkness and in the shadow of death, to guide our feet into the way of peace" (Luke 1:78-79). "For mine eyes have seen thy salvation, Which thou hast prepared before the face of all people; A light to lighten the Gentiles, and the glory of thy people Israel" (Luke 2:30-32).

The birth of Jesus Christ was accompanied by a great outshining of celestial light. A bright and radiant new star appeared to the Wise Men in the east to indicate that the long-awaited time had come. That same star appeared to them in the land of Judah and guided them to where the Christ Child was. The shepherds in the fields about Bethlehem were keeping their flocks by night when suddenly they were engulfed in a blaze of light as "an angel of the Lord stood by them, and the glory of the Lord shone round about them." *"The glory of the Lord shone round about them!"* The shepherds, the Wise Men, the mother and the patient saints were all witnesses to the light of the Lord which shone upon them and within their hearts at the coming of the Sun of Righteousness.

Turning to the testimony of one who walked for many years in the light of his Saviour and Lord, John the beloved disciple, we come to the sublime teaching of the Prologue to John's Gospel. Here we have the simplest and the profoundest interpretation of the meaning of the birth of Christ. Here we have the revelation of the true Light of Christmas. "In him was life; and the life was the light of men." This simple declaration contains twelve words of one syllable each. Three of these words are used twice in this brief sentence. So simply stated, it is nonetheless one of the most comprehensive and profound declarations of the Gospel. It may be likened unto another of John's great statements: "God is love." The meaning of the sentence is expressed in the words "life" and "light," both of which have their source "in him." The source of "life" is Christ, and His "life" becomes the "light of men." The divine resources contained in Christ, the eternal Word of God, are thus placed at the disposal of men. God's eternal purpose in His Son is to save mankind and glorify His holy name.

## I. *The Light of God.*

Christ is the light of men in the full, complete and perfect sense. He is the light that men need most. He is the light of revelation, the light of moral and spiritual truth, the light of salvation, the light of the soul, the light of the world, the light of heaven, the light of eternal life. "I am the light of the world:" He says, and "he that followeth me shall not walk in the darkness, but shall have the light of life." These words of Christ imply that the world is in darkness, that man's soul is in darkness apart from the illumination of the "true light" that has come into the world. He has come to be the light of the world and the light of the soul of every man who will receive Him.

The fundamental need of men is the light of God. This is affirmed by all who have had the truest insight into the nature and needs of humanity. It is demonstrated by all who have lived most worthily and usefully in the world. It is manifested most tragically yet unmistakably in the lives of those who deny, refuse and oppose this life-giving light. It is evidenced most plainly and pathetically in the confused, troubled, and sin-cursed condition of the world. The world of humanity perishes without the light of God, even as all physical life would perish without the light of the sun.

Christ brings the light of God to men. Christ reveals God the Father so that men may know Him, receive Him, love Him and serve Him. He reveals God the Father by the way of Incarnation, the fullest possible revelation that can be given to men in their mortal state. John says, "And the Word became flesh, and dwelt among us (and we beheld his glory, glory as of the only begotten from the Father), full of grace and truth." In his First Epistle he refers to Christ in similar terms: "That which was from the beginning, that which we have heard, that which we have seen with our eyes, that which we beheld, and our hands handled, concerning the Word of life." He, Christ, is God with us in human flesh, and yet the full glory of God has not been seen by the eyes of mortal man. "No man hath seen God at any time; the only begotten Son, who is in the bosom of the Father, he hath declared him." Thus Christ is "the final declaration, revelation, interpretation of the unseen God." He reveals the Father's sovereign glory, forgiving love, saving power and protecting care. He assures His people of the final revelation of God in glory; of fellowship with the God of light in Whom is no darkness at all. And in His glorious presence "there shall be night no more; and they need no light of lamp, neither light of sun; for the Lord God shall give them light: and they shall reign for ever and ever."

## II. *The Light of Truth.*

Christ's life is the light of men in that He is the light of moral and spiritual truth. We remember that He said, "I am the way, and the truth, and the life." He is the Way to the Father, the Source of Truth, the Fountain of Life. Those who do not accept the truth as it is in Jesus and walk therein are bound to walk in the darkness. Every man has some light. He has been endowed by his Maker with the light of reason and with the light of conscience. The light of reason and the light of conscience have enabled many to live in the world wisely, prosperously and successfully, that is, according to human standards. Many achieve greatness in business, politics, art, military affairs, philosophy and science who depend solely upon the light of reason and conscience. Many appear to live high moral lives apart from avowed allegiance to Him Who is the source of all moral truth. But those who believe that the light of nature is sufficient for the needs of the mind and heart and will, merely demonstrate the limitations of their accepted mentors of reason and conscience. They fail to perceive their lack because they reject the great facts of *revealed truth.*

The light of revelation is outside of and beyond the sphere of reason and conscience. Christ embodies in Himself a world of moral and spiritual truth that could never have been discovered by the mind of man. God has *revealed* His Person, His truth, His life through the life and work of His only begotten Son. Christ's claims establish His sovereignty in the realm of moral and spiritual truth, and He insisted that men must abide by His claims or be lost in the darkness of eternal night.

"When I am in the world, I am the light of the world," He said. Why, then, do not all men willingly and thankfully accept His light and walk in the light of the Lord instead of in the darkness of their own benighted faculties? Christ explained why this is true. "And this is the judgment, that the light is come into the world, and men loved the darkness rather than the light; for their works were evil. For every one that doeth evil hateth the light, and cometh not to the light, lest his works should be reproved. But he that doeth the truth cometh to the light, that his works may be made manifest, that they have been wrought in God." There is a moral element in belief. Those who accept Christ and walk in His light are loyal subjects of the Kingdom of Truth and devoted servants of the will of God. Those who reject Christ and walk in the darkness are subjects of the Prince of Darkness and are engaged in works that are evil. The rejection of Christ as the moral standard and Guide of life is the certain and final indication of the condition of a man's heart. He may *think* he is living the right kind of a moral life without Christ, but in taking such a stand he merely avows his unbelief and rejection of the True Light of Life.

This attitude of unbelief and rejection is anticipated in the Gospel of Christmas. Simeon's words to Mary indicated that the moral condition of men's hearts would be revealed by their acceptance or rejection of Jesus. And in the Prologue to John's Gospel we read the sad and tragic words: "He was in the world, and the world was made through him, and the world knew him not. He came unto his own, and they that were his own received him not." By His coming into the world Christ has become the "true light" for every man who will receive Him. He has manifested the life of God and the truth of God that men may see and hear and be saved. He has laid down His life in redeeming love that men might believe in Him as their Saviour and Lord. If men blind their own eyes to the light of the world and the true light of their own lives, theirs is the eternal darkness and irreparable loss.

### III. *The Light of Eternal Life.*

Christ is the true light of men in that He is the giver of eternal life. Christ has much to say concerning eternal life. His message is unique even as His offer of eternal life is unique. The authority back of His message and His offer is derived from God the Father. "Even as thou gavest him authority over all flesh, that to all whom thou hast given him, he should give eternal life" (John 17:2). "For God so loved the world, that he gave his only begotten Son, that whosoever believeth on him should not perish, but have eternal life" (John 3:16). The essence of eternal life consists in an experiential knowledge of God the Father as revealed through Jesus Christ. "And this is life eternal, that they should know thee the only true God, and him whom thou didst send, even Jesus Christ" (John 17:3). The one condition of receiving eternal life is faith in Christ. "He that believeth on the Son hath eternal life; but he that obeyeth not the Son shall not see life, but the wrath of God abideth on him" (John 3:36).

Christ has this life in Himself and transmits it to those who believe on Him. He is the Bread of Life. He gives the food "which abideth unto eternal life." He gives the water which becomes in the believer "a well of water springing up unto eternal life." His words convey the message which issues in eternal life to those who hear and receive it. "Verily, verily, I say unto you, He that heareth my word, and believeth him that sent me, hath eternal life, and cometh not into judgment, but hath passed out of death into life" (John 5:24). The believer's possession of this life is the safe-guard against the evils and perils of this world. "And I give unto them eternal life; and they shall never perish, and no one shall snatch them out of my hand" (John 10:28). The possession of this life guarantees the resurrection at the last day, escape from judgment and death, and the blessed estate of the righteous in the Father's kingdom. "I am the resurrection, and the life: he that believeth on me, though he die, yet shall he live; and whosoever liveth and believeth on me shall never die" (John 11:25-26). "For this is the will of my Father, that every one that beholdeth the Son, and believeth on him, should have eternal life; and I will raise him up at the last day" (John 6:40). "Come, ye blessed of my Father, inherit the kingdom prepared for you from the foundation of the world: . . . And . . . the righteous [shall go] into eternal life" (Matthew 25:34, 46).

Eternal life is not merely "everlasting" life. Eternal life is essentially a *quality* of life which by its nature endures for ever. Eternal life is the life of God the Father, the Son, and the Holy Spirit in the soul of the believer. No man possesses this life by nature, by heredity, nor by an act of will. He must be born again by the Spirit of God to receive it. He must exercise saving faith in the Lord Jesus Christ and receive from Him the gift of eternal life.

"In him was life; and the life was the light of men." His life is for us the light of salvation, the light of sustaining fellowship, the light of safe-guarding care, the light of resurrection, the light of victory over death, the light of heaven, the light of eternal blessedness, the light of glory. In His light shall we see light. This world, at the best, is filled with shadows, perplexities, and dark insoluble mysteries. The best any of us can do is to "see in a mirror, darkly." But then we shall see face to face, and know fully even as we are fully known.

Thus the Light of Christmas takes on a broader and fuller meaning when we consider its ultimate effect upon the destiny of our immortal souls. The first words in the Bible attributed to God are found in the first chapter of Genesis: "And God said, Let there be light: and there was light" (Genesis 1:3). The last words in the Bible attributed to the glorified Christ are these: "Yea; I come quickly." In the beginning, God's word of creative power lighted this universe with the sun, moon, and stars. In the fulness of time, the Incarnation of the eternal Word of God gave to humanity the Light of the spiritual world. In the last day, Christ's coming again in glory will reveal the perfect light of heaven to the righteous who have loved Him and looked for His appearing. May the Light of Christmas bring us and all men into the light of God's eternal day!